The Art of Ethics

Values and Ethics Series, Volume 7

The Art of Ethics
A Psychology of Ethical Beliefs

Elizabeth Z. McGrath

Loyola University Press
Chicago

Loyola University Press
3441 North Ashland Avenue
Chicago, Illinois 60657

Cover design by Nancy Gruenke

Library of Congress Cataloging-in-Publication Data

McGrath, Elizabeth Z.
    The art of ethics : a psychology of ethical beliefs /
Elizabeth Z. McGrath.
        p.   cm . — (Values and ethics series ; v. 7)
    Includes bibliographical references and index.
    ISBN 0–8294–0753–7 (hard)
    1. Ethics. 2. Ethics—Psychological aspects. I. Title.
II . Series : Values & ethics series ; v. 7.
BJ1012.M318   1993
170' . 1—dc20   93–36798
                                                        CIP

Contents

Introduction

If you were stopped on the street today by an interviewer, portable microphone in hand, and asked if you recycle, you, like most people, would probably reply, "Of course." And you could no doubt indicate the various materials you separate—glass, plastic, aluminum, and so on. And if, again like most people, you were questioned further about the effects of the nonbiodegradable substances on the planet, you could probably quote some of the staggering statistics about how long each plastic milk carton would prove a scourge to the environment. But if the interviewer then shifted the issue away from how to recycle and asked why we should recycle (not why in the sense of conserving our finite resources or making a public commitment to condemn waste, but rather why in the sense of acting ethically) you might find yourself at a bit of a loss. It is not that you do not know that it is wrong to waste, but when you seriously attempt to state just exactly why you hold that belief so strongly, you may find to your chagrin that the real reason you believe it is wrong to waste stems from that time back in second grade when you threw away a sandwich you did not like, and, when your teacher discovered your deed, she seized the moment to teach you the evils of wasting. You learned the lesson well—so well, in fact, that here you are, half a lifetime later, relying on your second grade teacher to justify one of your staunchly held ethical beliefs. Where does this leave you? With countless others! We have all absorbed our ethical beliefs from a wide variety of sources over a lifetime. Throughout the process we were not even aware that this conglomeration of beliefs was building up, much less that, because of the diversity of sources, we would eventually end up with what can only loosely be referred to as an ethical system—a set of beliefs whose members have as their only genuinely shared trait ownership by the same person.

It is unsettling to realize that issues to which we respond quite passionately and for which we are even willing, at times, to sacrifice dearly are so little understood and challenged by us. For most of us, our ethical beliefs represent the final frontier of our understanding. It is the last area we subject to critical analysis, and so, although these ideas dictate and control behavior in virtually every aspect of our lives, many of us will live and die understanding the internal workings of our VCRs more intimately than we do the internal workings of our ethical systems. Why would a naturally inquisitive species like Homo sapiens be so conspicuously lax in this particular area? The answer lies beneath our intellectual veneers, in almost primitive fears and taboos that prejudice and handicap us in even our meager efforts to learn and understand what ethics is all about.

An unnatural aura surrounds ethical truths. Most of us have come to accept, on both conscious and unconscious levels, that ethical rules, unlike any other body of information or system of guidelines, represent the will or plan of some sort of divine, or at least superhuman, agent. That agent is, by nature, so different from us mere mortals that we implicitly trust that the agent's brand of wisdom is right and compelling. Unlike a recipe for vegetable soup, which we may tinker with until we achieve the taste we most enjoy, we are taught from the time we are very little that ethical dictates must not be tampered with (or even questioned) to suit our tastes and preferences. We learn to distrust the standards by which we measure other sorts of assertions on the grounds that ethics is fundamentally different from every other sort of knowledge. It is consistently singled out and almost universally treated as a special subject that need not make sense in order to be reliable and trustworthy. Enshrining ethical knowledge with special status and unique epistemological priorities has perhaps stalled our inquisitiveness in this area, but that is really only half the problem.

If I, like Alice in Wonderland, were to confront a set of beliefs—a working system—that defied all the known rules of logic, that could not be questioned or challenged, and that required something akin to intellectual schizophrenia to juggle, I would have an interesting and perhaps temporarily entertaining puzzle, but one I would soon grow tired of and discard precisely because I could not use my intellectual powers to expand and energize or vivify it. We think and question precisely because knowledge empowers us to deal with reality. A topsy-turvy, fictional system may amuse briefly, but soon our interests turn back to what is useful and necessary, and we again seek knowledge for its life-value.

Our attachment to our topsy-turvy ethical systems is not just the intellectual acknowledgment that these beliefs defy human deciphering but is, even more so, the half-fear, half-belief that this sort of knowledge somehow reveals the ultimate standard of our worth as human beings. This implicitly held belief both scares us away from tinkering with the system and enslaves us to it. We are afraid to ask why and afraid to stray from the path, even though for most of us the paths multiply, diverge, and often lead to dead ends. If I fail at teaching, I may be branded by my students or peers as a bad teacher, but if I fail under my ethical belief system, I may be branded as a bad person—and that fundamental distinction makes all the difference psychologically. We are constantly encouraged from the time we are quite small to seek our own answers to questions about how plants grow, whether the stove is hot, how animals store food for the winter, and so on, but we are just as vigorously discouraged from exploring ethical knowledge. A mistake in the first example might leave you sadder but wiser, but a slip in ethics could leave you in hell (if your ethical beliefs were tied to certain religious doctrines) or at least declared a social misfit, outcast, or degenerate.

Many of us have stumbled along over the years, acquiring greater sophistication of thought and analysis and yet all the while directing that light anywhere except on our ethical views. If we now can free ourselves from our fears of total annihilation for daring to ask the questions, some inevitable uncertainties arise. How do I begin to go about evaluating my ethical beliefs? By what criteria can I judge? Who really are the experts? What have I meant all this time when I talked about my ethical beliefs?

Perhaps an even more basic question is Why think about ethics at all? Why even concern ourselves with these questions in the first place? The answer is that ethics is humanity's way of making sense of life, of the world, of the purpose of our being. Like it or not, we are conscious beings, and we do wonder about the world and our lives and the point of it all. We are driven, at least sporadically, to try to understand why we are here. Each of us wanders through the world, as one philosopher notes,

> with some kind of "moral squint." We focus. We scan. We search. We scrutinize. We stare. We give dirty looks. When we look into things, we may take close looks, quick looks, good looks, hard looks, long looks, or honest looks. We can look with favor or disfavor. We look around; we look askance; and we overlook things. We look down on people, up to people, and out for people. We speculate (literally spy out). We inspect, respect, and expect (originally *exspect*). With some linguistic license, we can say that we introspect, retrospect, circumspect, and prospect (for more than gold). More often than not, we see what we want to see. Sometimes, when our defenses are down, we get hit between the eyes with something we had no desire to see. . . . To borrow one of Stanley Hauerwas's titles, *vision and virtue* are two ways of talking about what makes us tick.[1]

We cannot get away from ethics because it is what makes us tick. We may try to ignore its significance and may even succeed for some time, but eventually each person experiences a crisis or challenge that requires him or her to try to make sense of it all. As William May puts it, ethical theories provide for us "corrective vision."[2] Life events are not just separate, disconnected moments that lack continuity and direction: we naturally search for the thread that will weave them all together and reveal the pattern behind the scenes and below the surface. The need to understand and make sense of life seems to be built into our hearts and minds. Ethics is the means of addressing the incessant *Why?*

To dispel some of the controlling fears and notions mentioned earlier, the first step should include detaching ethics from particular religious views, at least for our initial analysis. Ethics is a necessary component of most religious doctrines, but adherence to religious views is not a necessary component of being ethical and holding views on ethical matters. For the moment, we will limit our discussion to the human arena and address only those features that all ethical systems—religious and purely humanistic alike—have in common.

Examining Our Ethical Beliefs

Verifying and Falsifying Ethical Statements

> There are some people—and I am one of them—who think
> that the most practical and important thing about a man is
> still his view of the universe. We think that for a landlady
> considering a lodger it is important to know the man's
> income, but still more important to know the man's philoso-
> phy. We think that for a general about to fight an enemy it is
> important to know the enemy's numbers, but still more
> important to know the enemy's philosophy. We think the
> question is not whether the theory of the cosmos affects mat-
> ters, but whether in the long run anything else affects them.[1]

Ethical beliefs are beliefs about how things ought to be, but they
reflect certain beliefs about how things are. An *is* may never, as
Hume would say, make an *ought*, but our own beliefs about how
things should be and how life should be conducted will necessarily incorporate and reflect our beliefs about what is and what can
be. A person who believes, for example, that human beings are
totally determined by forces outside themselves—that they are, in
effect, the sum of forces that cannot be altered, deflected, or
channeled—will mean something very different by the phrase
"ethically correct behavior" than would a person who believes
that humans freely choose and shape their own personal des-
tinies. Which person is correct? This depends on what is meant
by the question: whose view of human nature is correct or whose
theory of ethics will work best, given the particular view of

human nature. Both seem to be reasonable questions as formulated and appear to bear on somewhat related issues. However, the two questions address radically different matters with respect to what human reason and epistemological method can establish and verify.

Epistemology is the field of philosophy that deals with questions about how we come to know the truth-value of an idea, how we recognize the truth when we see it, and what we mean when we say that our ideas are true or false; it explores all facets of human knowledge and understanding. When we address an issue as slippery as ethical truths, we must consider carefully how we use our words and notice that even the most common, familiar terms may undergo a subtle shift in meaning when applied to ethical beliefs or knowledge. The culprit here, and generally throughout ethical debates, is a linguistic one, not one of faulty data or sloppy analysis. Since ethical beliefs when formulated as statements look like other assertions of fact, it seems natural to question whether they, like other assertions of fact, are true or not. We desire to hold only true ethical beliefs and to cast off the false ones.

However, a cursory look at the truth-function of other statements is sufficient to reveal what is unique about truth-functions of ethical statements. Consider the simple example of my belief that it is raining outside and my concern about whether or not my belief is true. Testing my idea and verifying or falsifying it is a fairly simple matter: I can go to the window and observe what is happening and, if I believe that my view may be obscured by large trees, so that I might be unable to distinguish between rain falling and water dripping from the branches, I may go to a different window or I may go outside to check for myself. I might ask someone else who has recently come in from outdoors. The belief can be verified or falsified because it describes a state of affairs that either does or does not exist and that can be empirically verified. There are certain easily discernible differences between rain falling and rain not falling. Because I know what to expect outside the window if it is raining, I know how to tell if it is raining.

Consider now ethical beliefs. They, too, describe states of affairs, but not states that exist: they describe states that ought to exist. How do I verify a "fact" about what ought to be, but is not? For example, my belief that I should remove my grandmother from life support cannot empirically be proved true or false. Is it more ethical to sustain life at any cost, both financial and emotional, or is it more ethical to end suffering? I can test this belief only if I can figure out which is more ethical. Unlike empirical facts, which are about what does exist, ethical beliefs are about what ought to exist. If we try to use the terms *truth* and *verify* here in the same way as I did when I tested my belief that it was raining outside, we will not get very far. By its nature, an ethical belief does not describe reality, so what is the value of the belief? How could any such belief be true or false? What would truth-values of ethical beliefs mean? I suggest that the words *true* and *false* still apply, and that if the old model of truth as matching the picture (idea) with the reality is replaced with the model of a truth-function as a predictor, the terms will carry over smoothly from describing what is to describing what ought to be.

Unfortunately, in the English language we use the same word, *good,* to describe both emotionally pleasing acts or objects and morally correct ones. So ice cream is good and indignation over violations of due process is also good. And since my enjoyment of ice cream is largely a matter of personal taste and as such is a very private and immediate experience, I may well assume that concern about due process is likewise the result of highly personal feelings. If this assumption is followed to its logical conclusion, then we might believe that discussing differences of opinion about ethical issues would be as great a waste of time as an argument about whether ice cream or cake is the best dessert.

But, if we are going to treat ethical assertions as statements susceptible to study and analysis and argument, with at least some hope of understanding and resolving them, then some elements of ethical judgments must be objective or rational, that is, we can determine whether they are true or false. We assert that ethical judgments are objective when we make ethical assertions to others.

Unlike judgments that a pie is good or a movie is bad, statements such as "Genetic engineering is good" or "Child abuse is bad" are intended by us to express not only how we feel about the issue but also to dictate the way we think these matters should be viewed by others. This universal, compelling nature of ethical judgments is a unique characteristic of such beliefs. Unlike our feelings about banana cream pie, our feelings about genetic engineering or child abuse are matters about which we argue with others in an attempt to sway their opinions, should theirs differ from ours. Why we are willing and sometimes even anxious to pursue the matter with others is, in part, because we sense that such beliefs reveal more than our opinions, that they somehow reveal something about what is objectively right or wrong—facts—not only for us, but for everyone. We therefore might attempt to justify our ethical beliefs when they differ from others', a move we would never feel compelled to take on matters of taste, which do not bear this ethical character. The process becomes immediately complicated, however, as we attempt to verify and justify in the ethical sphere according to the logical rules that apply to empirical facts.

Ethical beliefs incorporate empirical data and interpretive data. From our experience with human drives, capabilities, and desires, we all have some knowledge of empirically verifiable facts about humans. Ethical theories describe how best to channel our drives, how best to direct our abilities, and how best to act on our desires. Ethical beliefs are value judgments that lend themselves to justification rather than to direct verification.

A social worker visiting the United States from an eastern European nation remarked how shocked and discouraged her peers who worked in her country's correctional system were by the dramatic increase of crime in their country. (Although they found the increase shocking, only one person in their entire country was serving a life-term in prison—the stiffest sentence, reserved for only the most serious crimes.) She explained that the source of their surprise was the lack of impact of the implementation of a communistic system in that nation. Those who accepted the assumption that private property is the root of all human evil had rather simplistically concluded that banishing private property would quickly end crime. Life did not bear out their expectations. The reality does not automatically falsify their belief that private property is an ethical evil and contributes to the downfall of humankind, but the facts seem to refute the idea that it is the sole cause of all human evil. A misunderstanding of how humans operate and respond is sufficient to skew an ethical system.

So, what does it mean to say that our ethical beliefs are true? Unlike assertions about reality that merely picture what is there, ethical assertions are expressions that incorporate (*a*) certain assumptions about humans and their nature, powers, and abilities, (*b*) logical rules that allow us to extrapolate from these assumptions, and (*c*) ethical beliefs, which represent a conclusion about what is desirable and good.

In William James's tribute to G. K. Chesterton quoted at the outset of this chapter, Chesterton points out the pervasive impact of a person's philosophy. The same sentiments could be expressed about a person's ethical system. When I consider loaning something of great value to another person, I am more interested in knowing the person's view of responsibilities and obligations to others than I am in whether or not the person would have enough money to replace the item should it be damaged or misplaced; if the person feels no obligation to take care of my belongings, how much money that person has is inconsequential. Our behavior is very much a function of our ethical beliefs. None of us is consistent, but the role of ethics as our internal monitor or supervisor is too notorious to dispute. Why it is not always successful in controlling us is examined at the end of our analysis.

How Ethical Belief Systems Parallel Mathematical Systems

If one were to compare ethical systems with mathematical systems, then the most basic and subjective elements of ethics, our intuitively felt beliefs about the way the world is, would be the axioms; our ethical assertions would be the theorems; and our justifications would be the logical rules by which we derive the theorems from the axioms. Questioning the truth-value of the result, our ethical beliefs, independently of the process by which we reached those theorems is fruitless and betrays a lack of understanding of the complexity of the process.

The first part of the analysis must be the examination of our axioms and the process by which we choose. The development of our axioms is the most basic function we perform as we begin to experience the world and see how it responds to us. To some extent we can describe these axioms as formulations of how we think the world is, but even that is a bit too intellectualized, because the axioms are only rarely consciously articulated, even to ourselves. A more apt description for most of our axioms would be an impression, rather than a formal belief, of how the world is and has been experienced.

I came across a conversation that illustrates this frustrating yet continuous process of acquiring axioms and arguing results, although the example was cited to present other, more obvious logical problems. Leo Buscaglia, a teacher and lecturer on love and human relationships, in a lecture that examines levels of meaning in our language, describes the emotional content of a phrase as the immediate sense we have of the referent, as opposed to the cognitive meaning, which is the term's objective meaning and which is shared by all who use our language on an adult, cognitive level. The following conversation, cited by Buscaglia to explain the notion of the subjective meaning of a phrase, shows an axiom choice and the theorem built on it by a young girl whose experience has led her to adopt a particular attitude (ethical theorem), which is challenged by an observer:

> I remember another young girl . . . when you mention the word *mother*—you know, to me [Buscaglia] it brings a smile on my lips and a wonderful warmth in my heart because I had an incredible lady called Mother. But this girl had a drunkard for a mother who used to pick people up and bring them in at night and lock her in the closet. And when somebody said, "Oh, honey, you should love your mother!" she said, "Why the hell should I?". . . And that was a good question.[2]

The observer's assertion that one should love one's mother represented a conclusion (ethical theorem) that came in response to an experience that probably differed drastically from the one experienced by the young girl. All of us have no doubt incorporated some ethical theorems on the say-so of another, even when the theorem conflicted with our internally determined consistent axioms and with our key experiences. We were not free to stick to our axioms and reject the authority that insisted on adopting the particular theorem.

In Buscaglia's example, the young girl demonstrates a certain logic and symmetry in her axioms and corresponding theorems. Is symmetry always desirable? What if experiences and emotional states (axioms) dictate ethical theorems that are detrimental to the individual or society or both? In other words, must the axioms be given priority if we are to create genuine, rationally based ethical systems? The answer is definitely no. Axioms are often adopted with as little critical reflection as are ethical theorems. Sometimes an incident early in one's life, intensely experienced, can so dominate one's impressions about life and getting along with others that there is no rational means of arguing against the impression. It blinds us to any other way of viewing these people or interactions. Emotional help is sometimes required to break the unhealthy grip that the axiom has on the individual and to correct the damage that such an axiom can inflict. The ineffective response of the observer in her attack on the young girl's ethical theorem now appears even more ridiculous, because she obviously failed to recognize that argument is not the vehicle by which she can reach the root of the girl's beliefs.

We reason from axioms, not to them, and so our most basic beliefs are generally not amenable to logical wrangling. People's choices of axioms are driven by nonrational forces responding to the ways in which the world has affected them. But with a little patience, anyone can identify and articulate those beliefs and so expose unrealistic, unbalanced, or simply biased or prejudiced axioms. These axioms truly are the root of the problem, but because they are beyond logic, they are usually unrecognized. They motivate the beliefs but are never answerable in a meaningful way. Because our ethical theorems are generally more public, more readily accessible, we are more likely to criticize and analyze them. However, they are only the conclusions in the process and, as the example indicates, are meaningless when challenged separately from the experiences that prompted them. If our theorems proceed logically from our axioms, they are virtually unassailable. If you cannot fault my reasoning in getting to square two, then the only way you can argue that my location is incorrect is to explain why I should have started from some spot other than square one.

Returning now to the person interviewed on the street who discovers a teacher's words still ringing in his or her ears, the dilemma created by her externally imposed theorems becomes more clear. We attempt to behave according to the dictates (theorems) of our system, but the theorems are only partially a response to our genuinely embraced and understood axioms and logical rules. At least some of our ethical beliefs are, no doubt, authentically formed and wholly subscribed to, but a vast number of equally compelling theorems were simply tacked on or forcefully appended from without, with no regard to how or whether they would logically fit the framework. And since we have accepted these additions uncritically, without an internal test for consistency, our theorems often contradict one another. We feel conflicting drives or moral ambivalence. When called to make an ethical response, we languish in the dilemma with no ready guide to sort out the mess. All alternatives are perceived as equally compelling and, without logical tools to discriminate, no clearly best answer is discernible.

The example of the person being interviewed points out the critical role our ethical beliefs play: they dictate behavior and guide our actions when we are placed in certain contexts and are forced to act. Which contexts and which actions become clear as we consider the sources and reliability of our axioms, our logical rules, and, finally, the result: our ethical beliefs.

Choosing Our Axioms

To even speak of choosing axioms is to make explicit an axiom shared by those who bother to discuss the creation, maintenance, and justification of ethical systems, that is, the axiom that choice is a reality. The process of choosing axioms may be conducted with greater or lesser degrees of reflection or consciousness, but unless we have a real choice all the talk about ethics is a waste of breath. Responses like blinking or flinching when one perceives an impending blow are not labeled ethical or unethical but are merely nonethical precisely because they are automatic and are not behaviors that one can control or choose. And if one believes that a murderer's act of pulling the trigger and causing the death of another is as automatic and uncontrollable, then that act will likewise lose its ethical character.

Choosing is a very complicated process. It includes incorporating axioms, developing logical rules, compiling ethical theorems, and, finally, choosing when to observe the theorems or rules. Choices are being made constantly, but few are noticed or analyzed. From society's standpoint, if a person kills another, the only choice really examined in any depth is the one at the end of the chain: did the individual choose to act in defiance of society's ethical theorems? Like the observer responding to the young girl, we address the end of the process in the vain hope of rooting out the problems that were built in at the beginning. Ethical beliefs are not a simple matter of declaring certain acts to be right or wrong or of identifying individuals as innocent or guilty.

How and why we make the choices we do becomes clear only through a great deal of work in unearthing the sources of some of our most cherished beliefs and our orientation toward life and toward others. Why do some people, despite very difficult and trying lives, continue to look for the best in others? What choice does this represent? Why do some people choose to believe that there is something more going on in the universe than what is visible in the natural sphere and hence adopt belief in some spirituality or religion? The variety in responses may reflect temperament, disposition, or environment. Family traits play out their constructive or destructive effects on the individual and his or her ethical views.

But dispositions and tendencies need not be controlling and condemning. Unlike genetic coding for eye color, our predispositions to act in certain ways seem to respond to choice and can be redirected or, if necessary, overridden. We cannot be certain of this response because psychology cannot absolutely verify the accuracy of the felt experience, but ultimately we all simply feel that we are free to make at least some choices. Rejecting that basic principle, despite the fact that it would solve all our ethical dilemmas by proving that ethics as we know it is illusory, would leave us with an even more distressing and fundamentally unacceptable principle to grapple with: that we have no control over our actions and that our autonomy is, in fact, illusory. I would in that case cease to be ethically blameworthy for bad behavior, but, likewise, I would also no longer be ethically praiseworthy for good behavior. In fact, I would no longer be steering the ship, so to speak. What I would have formerly referred to as my *self* would be merely the locus of converging forces that form *me*. I do not have the expertise to settle the age-old free-will-versus-determinism debate, but I believe that if one is to wrestle with ethical questions, this act supposes that one must profess or hold a belief in some genuine autonomy and choice on the part of each ethical individual.

William James addressed the havoc that is wreaked upon one's belief system by the impact of complete determinism. If one is truly not free to choose, then the agony one experiences in facing an ethical dilemma is both necessary and futile because it is predetermined. One's commitment to act in one way or another is really just an acknowledgment of the inevitable, not a purposeful act. The regrets that follow when one perceives that one has chosen poorly are also futile and yet necessary. The analysis does not disprove the validity of the doctrine of determinism, but it points out the series of beliefs that are inevitably upset by the shift in one key axiom.

Thus, if one adopts the initial axiom that we humans do make genuine choices, then the first and most basic choices we make would include discovering the axioms of our beliefs. And because these choices precede the development of any sophisticated logical apparatus or mode of verification, the axioms are selected or chosen on nonrational or, in some cases, irrational grounds. The axioms often represent our attempt to make sense of data that has been thrust upon us. We adopt the impression that makes the most sense as a working hypothesis, and that impression of the data becomes our accepted version of that reality. The axioms settle in our minds how to incorporate the flux of data and how that data can be shown to be compatible with numerous conflicting theories.

How and why we make the selections we do is itself an interesting problem but more properly an epistemological question and therefore outside the purview of this work.

John Hick, in his classic anthology on the philosophy of religion, includes a short article by John Wisdom entitled "Gods," which illustrates how belief or lack of belief in God represents a response—call it interpretation or perhaps creation of a hypothesis—to ambiguous data.[3] In the story, two people in a long-neglected garden discover among the many weeds a number of apparently cultivated flowering plants. One observed that a gardener must be working there because the flowers would not have survived without some attention. The other stated the opposite thesis: that there could certainly not be any gardener tending the plot because no gardener would allow the weeds to have taken so firm a hold. Since they did not test the competing hypotheses, the issue, of course, was never and could never be resolved. What is evident from this story, however, is that two observers could see the same data—the weeds and the flowers—but reach a completely different and contradictory conclusion about the data's significance and relative value. The theory of each observer was based on that portion of the data that was perceived as most compelling. Wisdom's point, of course, is that we "select" our basic beliefs as we unconsciously confront incomplete data and, by emphasizing one part over another, formulate our beliefs about the whole.

In addition to the choices that we make as we build from the bottom up, so to speak, we also incorporate axioms that come to us from the top down. We inherit these tenets from every social institution, starting with our families, that contains and educates us. Some of the socially imposed axioms come to us as facts and theories, while others come to us indirectly. We absorb certain attitudes of trust or distrust, tolerance or narrowness, prejudice or open-mindedness, and these attitudes in turn inform our later choices. As we set our patterns of choosing, we are less likely to consider alternative approaches or pay attention to conflicting data. We hope our axioms build on one another to form a unified network of beliefs and attitudes, but intense experiences may disrupt our pattern of selection and absorption so that a single axiom can wield such authority that it can generate many theorems and behaviors, while we are unaware of its source.

A marvelous example of how the axioms direct behavior and support our theorems is presented by Thomas Davis in his book in which he teaches philosophical concepts through works of fiction—in this case science fiction—and the result is a precise working model of the process of how knowledge (a field of axioms) translates into attitudes and behavior.

Davis's story entitled "Those Who Help Themselves" describes the destruction by earthlings of a civilization on a distant planet. Our history has been a long chronicle of destruction and brutality directed by one group toward another, but what distinguishes this conflict is revealed when the commentator notes, "We have just destroyed what may be the only truly moral civilization that ever existed."[4]

Such a tribute draws the reader in as the author reveals his impressions of this extraterrestrial race. I must admit that, just as Davis hoped his readers would, I found myself somewhat defensive as well as curious about what made these beings capable of achieving the truly moral civilization we humans have failed to accomplish through our stumbling efforts at interpersonal relations and advancing as civilized, socialized beings. The doomed race, the Omegans, were corporeal beings with roughly the same structure and sensory apparatus that we have. They evidently experienced the same intellectual and emotional development that our species has. So their organic structure did not explain their moral superiority. They had minds, feelings, the ability to choose, and all the internal struggles and conflicts that we face.

If the difference could not be discerned in their structure, the next place to look was their environment. One explanation for human greed and lack of ethical development is that humans have always competed for resources. This competition creates the ill will and distrust that make ethical behavior self-defeating and therefore unlikely. But Davis's species again paralleled our own in that they lived with scarcity and competition.

Since differences in organic or environmental factors were small, the last easy explanation, religion, was examined. Religion has played a prominent role in the development of each human culture's ethical system, so the commentator naturally questioned the Omegans on their metaphysical beliefs. To his (and the readers') disappointment, he could find no significant difference in the way the Omegans approached religion and the way humans do. For example, the Omegans disagreed about the existence of a divine being. Whether they believed strongly or not at all seemed to have little impact on the individual Omegan's conduct.

After exhausting the usual determinants of ethical beliefs, the commentator stumbled upon a belief (an axiom) held by all members of the culture, irrespective of religious affiliation, that fully explained their highly ethical behavior: all the Omegans believed, without any physical proof or religious revelation, in reincarnation. Unlike the reincarnation that many human religions espouse, in the Omegans' theory placement of a soul into a new body was totally random. It in no way reflected how good or how bad one had been. Therefore, helping someone less fortunate than oneself took on a distinctly selfish dimension, since one might easily be less fortunate in the future. Helping others was helping oneself. Although humans tolerate incredible poverty alongside fantastic wealth, the Omegans were not comfortable with such wide disparities because, although one might be in the wealthy class on this trip through life, the next time one might not be so lucky.

One might argue that the Omegans were not truly morally superior to humans after all. Like us, their acts were the products of selfish motives. However, their behavior, which was benevolent toward every other Omegan, was indistinguishable from benevolent behavior rooted in purely unselfish desires and drives.

If one is judging the ethical quality of an act by the motive, regardless of the outcome, then the Omegans would prove as frail ethically as do we humans. However, if one judges the ethical quality of behavior by the nature and effect of the behavior, then good deeds done for whatever reason become ethically good and therefore desirable acts. Motives function prominently in the second phase of belief formation—the creation of logical rules and rational projection. But the Omegans' axiom undeniably prompted their treatment of one another, and such institutionally established or endorsed notions (axioms) create widely implemented norms of behavior and influence large groups of people who may never realize the link between the rather vague concept and their own actual behavior.

In the latter part of the nineteenth century, sociologist Harriet Martineau, who is credited with formalizing the methodology of sociological research, wrote *How to Observe Morals and Manners* to teach sociologists and outsiders how to learn, through observation and interaction, about the moral beliefs of other cultures and compensate for the filtering process that our own culturally indoctrinated beliefs create. Martineau shows how a culturally adopted axiom can influence the behavior of an entire people in a dangerous way through a story about the queen of Spain. The queen was mounting her horse when it bolted and her foot became entangled in the stirrup. According to Spanish custom, no one other than the queen's personal pages were allowed to touch her person, particularly her feet, but the pages were young boys and were too small to help. As the king watched from the residence, several adult servants stood dutifully by, not daring to lay a hand on the queen's feet, until two of them risked the king's wrath to save her life and managed to extricate her foot. Then they fled for their own lives, fearing the judgment of the king. And in response to the rather curious behavioral rule that no one except the pages can touch the queen's foot Martineau says: "Whence such a law? From the rule that the queen of Spain has no legs. Whence such a rule? From the meaning that the queen of Spain is a being too lofty to touch the earth. Here we come at last to the sentiment of loyal admiration and veneration which sanctifies the law and the rule, and interprets the incident."[5] She comments that to an outsider such a rule would appear a "solemn absurdity," but to the believers the noble sentiment could not yield any other behavior.

Every group of believers will be able to find, if they examine their axioms, similar examples of behavioral dictates that, upon close inspection, seem inappropriate and sometimes even dangerous. Choosing axioms is the first critical step in creating an ethical belief system, and, to be effective, analysis of one's system must include careful examination of as many axioms as one can identify. The second step in the process is how one uses those axioms: creating logical rules for developing ethical theorems.

Creating Logical Rules

Our logical rules represent our means of justifying our ethical theorems (rules for behavior). Consider how you could defend your answers to the following questions:

1. Is murder morally wrong? Why or why not?
2. If you could steal a million dollars in such a way that no one would ever know that you were the thief and no one would ever suffer from the loss of the money, would you be morally wrong to steal it? Why or why not?

Justifications for ethical views generally follow one of two lines of reasoning: (1) the ethical value stems from the consequences of the action or (2) the ethical value stems from whether the action conforms to a law or standard. The former approach typifies a utilitarian, or relativistic, approach to ethics in which an act is judged by its consequences. The latter approach typifies an absolutist approach in which the code, law, or standard dictates the ethical character of the actions regardless of the results.

The utilitarian approach measures an act's ethical character according to strictly human standards—the greatest good for the greatest number—whether *good* is interpreted to mean happiness, pleasure, well-being, or some other human benefit. The absolutist approach, on the other hand, places the origins of the ethical law outside the sphere of strictly human endeavors and views humans as obligated to conform to this external standard—to something greater than humankind. And the chief aim of the authority that imposed this standard, be that authority nature, or God, or some intermediate being, may well not include happiness or pleasure at all, in that ethically correct acts could logically diminish pleasure for everyone. Since our whims and desires are not the supreme value, there is no guarantee that anyone will be left the happier for everyone having acted ethically.

Both lines of reasoning have definite strengths and weaknesses, and we may invoke one to cover some questions and the other to cover the remaining ones, although the choice is often unclear. Patterns of choice become more obvious as an individual examines how values were typically transmitted in his or her home, school, church, synagogue, mosque, or other institution.

Consider, for example, arguing that murder is wrong because of the painful consequences to the victim and the victim's family and friends. This concern over consequences indicates a utilitarian approach to the question. Furthermore, even if one were to derive pleasure from the act of murder itself or from the death of a particular person, by balancing the positive consequences to us against the negative consequences to the victim, we would usually say that the overall consequences would be so bad that the act would be morally wrong.

If, on the other hand, we maintain that murder is always wrong because we do not have a moral right to take another's life, we are taking an absolutist position, and our focus on rights, with no mention of consequences, indicates a standard that stands outside the act by which one can judge actions regardless of who or how many are helped or hurt by the action. Why one adopts a utilitarian or an absolutist posture depends on the action as well as the justification for it. Alternative justifications are considered shortly.

The second problem posed above, concerning the theft of a million dollars, has no blatantly bad consequences, because the thief would not be caught and no one would suffer from the loss of the money. For some, no bad consequences means no ethical problems, but for many others there would still be something ethically wrong with that action. The absolutist has no difficulty condemning the theft because the act is a violation of the natural law, or religious dictates, or whatever body of law he or she bases his or her ethical system on. The theft is wrong because a person has no right to the money, even if no one is hurt. However, because there are apparently no bad consequences, for many utilitarians the act is not morally wrong.

The utilitarians who do not endorse this act will claim that there really are bad consequences flowing from it, namely, the thief has been corrupted by his deceit and undeserved gain.

We all move back and forth between the extreme utilitarian position and the extreme absolutist one, but we commonly place greater dependence on one or the other. The following features of each position should be considered when one is trying to justify one's tendencies.

That absolutists place the source of ethical beliefs beyond one's likes or dislikes implies that we receive from our society some superhuman, perhaps even divine, fiat. This fiat seems to remove much uncertainty and ambiguity and imparts a feeling of belonging to a universal or eternal order; however, we must question the source of the fiat and of our certainty that we have properly understood it. Absolutism appeals to one's sense of order and purpose and overarching plan and to one's desire for security and safety, but as one matures and begins to question and exercise independent judgment one may find one has less confidence in absolutes that are not susceptible to this questioning. Absolutists frequently abandon the discourse about ethics because once they move beyond the human, empirical level into the realm of laws and absolutes, they and their opponents have no common ground for discussion. What is now profitable for discussion is an examination of the absolutists' basis for belief in this or that particular code or value; that discussion can reveal the wisdom or folly of clinging to perceived certain knowledge or ultimate law.

Utilitarians feel that they have escaped the rigidity of the absolutists' position but often find that they have traded an excessively rigid structure for one that offers too little support. To ground ethical values in the principle of the greatest good for the greatest number seems so obviously desirable that all disagreement should cease, but just what constitutes a good now becomes the issue. Several classical philosophers, such as John Stuart Mill, who attempted to schematize the utilitarian approach, measured goods with respect to intensity and duration. The resulting measure of pleasure seems contrived and artificial. The utilitarians' position appears more concrete, human, and manageable than the absolutists', but on close examination it reveals its own Achilles' heel. Proponents of each theory contend with the shortcomings of their position.

In the end, we feel the uncomfortable inkling that a reliable but flexible standard is the answer. Such a standard is yet to be widely articulated so the bad news is that we, like the billions who have lived before us, must learn to live and function with ambiguity. The good news is that, although not infallible, justification within each individual's system is possible. When one understands, freely embraces, and articulates a belief system, one admits that one is responsible for the values and rules by which one lives and fashions one's behavior. The notion of a freely chosen and thoroughly understood set of rules does not imply that each individual must refuse to benefit by the ideals and standards that others have articulated. Our errors have not generally come from relying on others' wisdom but rather from embracing beliefs that we have not examined. This conflict creates chaos and confusion, and we find ourselves without useful information and direction.

Behind our tendency to choose either to be guided by consequences or rules in ethical debates lies a trust in one or more methods of arriving at our ethical answers. And the bases we select to justify our judgments determine why this or that judgment is ultimately right or wrong. Who or what we trust to guide us is the ultimate arbiter.

Bases for Ethical Judgments

A perceived need for justification is one of the compelling features that distinguishes value judgments from judgments about purely subjective states. If I assert that I am in great pain, a reply from a listener that I should prove or justify that statement would seem absurd. A statement of such a personal and subjective nature should not require justification to anyone else. But the statement that date rape is "not all that serious" might well be challenged by someone expecting an objective justification. The justification one offers others differs with the subject matter, but the question of reliability is nonetheless central to deciding among competing ethical theories or assertions.

It is disconcerting to realize when challenged, even in a friendly way, in the midst of a conversation that we are not sure of the basis of our beliefs. If we try to trace our beliefs (ethical theorems) back to the underlying axioms, we may be shocked to find that our beliefs are actually unjustifiable. If we find that we simply cannot identify the basis of a belief through conscious effort, it helps to argue with an imaginary opponent and note what surfaces through the rationalization process. Only when we are confronted do many of us have the opportunity to examine the bases of our beliefs, and the defenses we offer are only as sound as the bases on which we rely. Of course, all bases have limitations, and all can be misapplied and misinterpreted, but they are the foundation of our individual ethical systems and are the starting point for useful debate. The bases we identify through self-examination probably fall into one or more of the following categories, although this is not an exhaustive list: authority, intuition and emotion, logic and reason, and empirical evidence.

Authority

Appeal to authority can be a very sound, rational move provided the authority is operating within the realm of his or her expertise and provided the authority is correctly formulating judgments. A common fallacy is appealing to an authority who offers a judgment outside his or her field. A simple example of this misuse of authority is interviewing movie stars about their opinions on United States foreign policy or perhaps the latest theory on the origin of the universe. This is not to suggest that actors are necessarily unknowledgeable about these subjects, but rather that their high status as movie stars does not guarantee their reliability in politics or cosmology. We often rely on the opinions of people we admire greatly for their knowledge or insight in one subject and then, unwittingly, we presume that they are equally reliable in others. In short, reliance on authority in making judgments is not categorically right or wrong, but its reliability in any particular case depends on the integrity and expertise of the authority, and often we do not (or perhaps cannot) really determine that.

The best protection against misuse of authority is a willingness to subject all beliefs, regardless of their source, to one's own scrutiny and analysis. One is much safer to be slow to adopt beliefs, despite the reputation or manner of the authority endorsing them, because it can be difficult to sort out error after it has been introduced into one's system.

Intuition and Emotion

Intuitive and emotional responses to ethical dilemmas are frequently used as the basis for belief. Intuition and emotion are not meaningless and useless; they often guide us to acts of kindness or altruism. But to test the ethical correctness of beliefs based solely on intuition or emotion requires a serious and profound look at the sources of these feelings and a rigorous scrutiny of the implications of adopting such beliefs. To depend solely, or even predominantly, on emotions or intuition for guidance is dangerous practice for two reasons. First, the individual has no rational means of assuring that these emotionally or intuitively based beliefs are more ethically correct than, say, Archie Bunker's sincere but prejudiced beliefs about the relative value of the races or sexes. These two sets of beliefs may be identical with respect to intensity of feeling, yet no one would want to espouse the idea that as long as one is sincere and feels deeply one must be right. Second, the individual has no common ground with others that can serve as a basis for discussion. The basis of one's beliefs is entirely personal and subjective and therefore does not lend itself to objective analysis. Carefully studying one's ethical belief system is finding those elements that have eluded analysis, rooting out suspect beliefs and leaving a system that is fully understood and to which one can freely and intelligently assent. Belief based solely on strong feelings is as anti-intellectual an approach as belief based solely on authorities.

Logic and Reason

A third basis commonly cited for ethical beliefs is logic or reason. If we think that our ethical beliefs are reasonable, it would seem to logically follow that other reasonable people will recognize and accept their truth-value as well. But appeal to logic is tricky because it invokes our highest faculty, as defined by philosophers. To assert that reason dictates that an action is ethically correct is no more compelling than to assert that an action is ethically correct because it is emotionally supported or dictated. Reasoning may be sound or unsound; it may proceed from true axioms or false ones. Reasoning is a sure method of moving from Point a to Point b, but if Point a is not the correct starting point, then we cannot know whether Point b is where we ought to end. Reasoning is a complicated and multifaceted process. To effectively appeal to reasoning as a basis for ethical belief requires patience and skill to analyze the process into its many steps and then examine their reliability. In short, this method, when properly understood and carefully used, is very reliable and can be thoroughly verified and analyzed. However, when most of us appeal to logic or reason in our ethical debates, we generally have not traced our beliefs back to their sources or made the careful examination to justify the procedure, and our conclusion that our beliefs "just make sense" is not truly an appeal to logic but is frequently merely another way of saying "it feels right to me."

Empirical Evidence

The last basis to consider is empirical evidence. Like logic, empirical evidence occupies a position of great respect and trust in the twentieth-century person's mind. We connect empirical evidence with science and science with totally objective truth. But the domain of science is all that is and, theoretically, all that can be, while the domain of ethics is primarily what should be. Correct ethical judgments require an understanding of what we, as humans, are and what our capabilities may be; but once we leave the realm of the *ares* and begin to consider the *oughts*, the usefulness of empirical data becomes decidedly limited. Appeals to empirical evidence can, when properly applied, shore up arguments about what we need for survival or physical well-being. Our understanding of the extent of our ability to will and choose and act affects our notions of what should be expected of us. For example, we do not hold a mentally disabled person responsible for his or her actions. Sufficient understanding and freedom from compulsion are empirical states necessary for ethical action, but they are not sufficient to determine whether our choices are ethical. I cannot act ethically without freedom, but not all free acts are ethical ones.

These bases—authority, intuition and emotion, logic and reason, and empirical evidence—are those most commonly cited in debates over ethical views. Each of them, when used properly and with its limitations in mind, has a place in the process, but each also has shortcomings that become apparent when we expect them to bear the full load of justifying our ethical views. No basis is either useless or entirely conclusive, but the way each is applied largely determines the reliability of the particular foundation of belief. The success or failure of the application reflects the skill, sincerity, and integrity of the believer.

By now our uncertainty in justifying our ethical judgments should be obvious, but equally obvious should be our ability to control the filtering processes that sort out our ethical beliefs and commitments with little, if any, active participation and control on our part. We need not be bound by a collection of unsolicited, unexamined, and unchallenged rules or commands. However, creating a consciously chosen and endorsed system of ethical beliefs requires an open and courageous intellectual stance coupled with a willingness to scrutinize and perhaps even reject some judgments that heretofore may have functioned as the cornerstone of a complex system of attitudes. Receptivity to and capability for such a project is the topic to be addressed next.

Evaluating Levels of Ethical Maturity

Rules, Authorities, and Ethical Development

Jean Piaget, a pioneer in researching the development of children's intellectual, emotional, and psychological capacities, prepared a study of the development of moral judgment in children. He chose as his focus the children's understanding and appreciation of rules because, as he notes, "all morality consists in a system of rules, and the essence of all morality is to be sought for in the respect which the individual acquires for these rules."[1] Unfortunately, by the time we are able to question intellectually the validity of particular ethical beliefs, we have already been emotionally programmed to respond to authority in ways that we do not even recognize, and thus we are conditioned to internalize rules automatically. Since an ethical overhaul requires breaking away from the established pattern of automatically accepting externally imposed rules, we need an understanding of the psychological import of these rules and the power that they exert over us on the subconscious level. We must learn to respond to the rules in a healthier way by evaluating their worth for us.

As Piaget points out, children are introduced to myriad rules and regulations and obligations that are stipulated by their parents even before they are capable of grasping the linguistic meaning of these rules. Children are generally issued the rules and forced to comply. The situations that reveal the most about the process of understanding and coping with rules, according to

Piaget, are those in which children interact with and respond to the rules voluntarily. The situation Piaget chose was a group of children learning to play marbles. Playing marbles may not seem similar to adopting an ethical belief system, but both activities include coping with externally dictated rules and regulations that one must either accept and follow or reject and face ostracization.

Piaget noted three observations at the outset of the study: (1) within any single group or locale there was always more than one accepted version of the game of marbles, a fact that at times weakened and at times strengthened some children's belief in the sacredness of rules; (2) each version of the game incorporated rules that differed from the rules in force when the children's parents or even older siblings played the game, and some older children Piaget interviewed actually bemoaned the passing of the rules that they had learned, as if the replacement of those rules indicated a deterioration of the game; and (3) even within a single game and in a single locale the children acknowledged that certain rules could be changed by group consensus.[2]

What is interesting about these phenomena is the impact that altering the rules has on the children's evaluation of the actions governed by those rules. Consider, for example, the appropriate response when a player mistakenly puts down a marble of superior value to replace an ordinary marble. The mistake, an easy enough one to make, could be immediately noticed and acknowledged by the player who made the mistake. Then he or she could simply pick up the marble and replace it with a marble of appropriate value. For an opponent to move quickly and capture the erroneously placed marble before the first player noticed would be considered dishonest and unacceptable behavior. In fact, Piaget notes that when children were queried about this tactic, each felt that such an underhanded move would be tantamount to stealing. However, if the player making the mistake did not recognize the error in a reasonable length of time, the opponent could then utter the word "toumike" or "toumikemik," and the marble would be declared fair game, the first player would lose the right to switch the marbles, and the opposing player would gain the right to capture the marble fairly.[3] This example reveals the power of formalism to transform the meanings that we attach to actions. Simply moving in on the mistakenly placed marble would be wrong, but a formal vehicle could transform that action into a right and appropriate move. The power of pronouncements to color the quality of actions is the basis of rules: actions become right or wrong as a result of how they are described and who makes the pronouncement.

What appears to be a simple children's game becomes a very complex exchange with decidedly ethical overtones. Issues of fairness, justice, and charity color some of the patterns but are always tied into the formal requirements that there be rules, that they be pronounced by someone designated as capable of asserting them, and that there be a general assent by the players to abide by the rules. These features emerge as fundamental aspects of all rule-governed behavior, of which ethical systems compose only a subclass.

How We Begin to Understand Rules

Piaget divided the development of a child's view of the practice and application of rules into four discernible stages.[4] The very young child acts and plays individually, unconcerned with who wins or even whether there is a winner. The child simply plays as his or her desires and motor skills allow. At this stage the child is not capable of grasping rules or purposes to activities, so he or she really does not participate in games per se but rather just plays on his or her own, using game pieces. At this earliest stage the activity is too subjective and individualized to be called rule-governed behavior.

In the second stage, the child begins to copy what older children are doing but remains somewhat oblivious to the bigger picture of competing to win. Because the young child does not understand competition, he or she may declare everyone the winner or simply lapse into private playing again. The child may grasp the significance of being declared the winner without understanding how one wins. For example, if he or she, without being blindfolded, successfully pins the tail on the donkey, he or she may declare, "I'm the winner!" because he or she does not know the rules of the game. Rules define not only the object of the game but also the acceptable way to win.

The third stage, which the child enters about the age of seven or eight years, is marked by cooperation. The child now plays with others and desires to play the real game and to really win. An understanding and codification of the rules begins to be important, because the child wants to know what to do to win. The purpose behind the rules is still vague to the child, but the rules become quite important as the child seeks to interact in a more organized way with others.

In the final stage, attained at roughly eleven or twelve years of age, the child becomes preoccupied with knowing the rules and with making the rules clear to others as well. The rules begin to take on a special significance because they control the child's games. A child spends much time in explaining the rules and codifying them for future games.

Equating Ethical Behavior with Obedience

This increased emphasis on knowing, understanding, and obeying the rules in playing parallels the children's emerging sense of right and wrong. Being good, or doing the right thing becomes associated in children's minds with being obedient, regardless of the rules or their sources. This association of ethical goodness with obedience is further strengthened in the Judeo-Christian tradition, for example, by the story in Genesis of the first sin. In the story, the sin that resulted in the banishment of our species from paradise for all time is the sin of disobedience. That the first human beings ate from the tree of knowledge is not treated as an intrinsically wrong act. The first sinful act was sinful because it was an act of disobedience. Consequently, people in the Judeo-Christian tradition tend to believe that the intrinsic value or character of an action is not necessarily related to its ethical character. As in the game of marbles, the act's acceptability can be judged only when one knows who pronounced it to be right or wrong. The pronouncement gives it its ethical character.

In *Being and Education,* Donald Vandenberg proposed an alternative model of education that would, by design, avoid the pitfall of current educational practices that stress the metamorphosis of children into obedient, socially conditioned beings above all else. In Vandenberg's view, the teacher bears the ethical obligation to help children preserve their integrity as individuals striving to be independent, and to resist the strong temptation to play on children's need for acceptance by exacting obedience as the price for approval.

> The responsibility and authority that the teacher has for the child is extremely significant. . . . Trust in the parents colors the appearance of his teachers, who have his confidence with or without meriting it. . . . This makes the teacher morally responsible for the child in yet another sense: the child is very susceptible to seduction, to having his being for others rather than for himself, no matter what he does. . . . Learning how to print a particular letter for its own sake and then showing it to the teacher to share the joy can be distinguished from learning to print the letter in order to avoid punishment and/or to derive joy from showing it to the teacher. The latter illustrates the seductiveness of the teacher that the child is open to and for which the teacher is morally responsible. . . . Room for disobedience is the safeguard against encroachments of the inauthentic use of authority that occur when the teacher lets herself fall away from herself in her being as a teacher.[5]

Much of our society's concept of ethics is a variant on the idea of obedience to authority. Many actually equate acting in an ethical manner with obedience to someone or some institution, so that the emphasis shifts away from the command itself to compliance and obedience to the command, often with little or no regard for its content. We may even experience guilt at disobeying an authority figure, whether or not we agree with that person's value judgments or pronouncements. The sheer act of disobeying creates anxiety and guilt, evoking the emotions we experienced as children when we disobeyed our parents and risked their disapproval, anger, punishment, or even their rejection and withdrawal of love.

A classic experiment measuring this phenomenon was conducted in 1964 by Stanley Milgram at Yale University. This modern-day morality tale, as R. D. Laing has described it, occurred as follows:[6]

Dr. Milgram recruited 40 male volunteers who believed they were to take part in an experimental study of memory and learning at Yale University. The 40 men were between the ages of 20 and 50 and represented a wide range of occupations. Typical subjects were postal clerks, high school teachers, salesmen, engineers and laborers. One subject had not finished elementary school, but some others had doctorate and other professional degrees. The role of experimenter was played by a 31-year-old high school teacher of biology. His manner was impassive but he maintained a somewhat stern appearance during the experiment. The experimenter was aided by a mild-mannered and likable man, who acted as a "victim." The experimenter interviewed each volunteer and, with him, the "victim" masquerading as another volunteer. He told the two of them that the intention was to investigate the effects of punishment on learning, and in particular the differential effects of varying degrees of punishment and various types of teacher. The drawing of lots was rigged so that the volunteer was always the teacher and the "victim" was always the learner. The victim was strapped into an "electric chair" apparatus and electrode paste and an electrode were applied. The teacher-volunteer was then taken into an adjacent room and placed before a complex instrument labeled "Shock Generator." The teacher-volunteer was given a 45-volt shock to demonstrate the apparent authenticity of the machine.[7]

The teacher-volunteer was told that he would be directed by the authority in charge of the experiment to administer increasingly more severe shocks to the learner-victim when the learner-victim gave incorrect responses to the questions directed to him. Supposedly the effect of negative reinforcement on the learner-victim's ability to respond correctly to questions could then be measured and analyzed. The responses of the learner-victim had actually been prearranged so that he consistently gave incorrect answers to three out of every four questions, and the teacher-volunteer was directed to continually increase the voltage of the shocks, despite the learner-victim's protests and responses, which ranged from kicking on the wall and moaning to feigned unconsciousness.

The results of the Milgram experiment were a complete surprise to all concerned, especially Milgram, who noted that he
observed poised, mature, educated men reduced to nervous
wrecks on the brink of breakdown because they were unable
emotionally to say no to the person they perceived to be in
authority. Twenty-six of the forty volunteers continued the
experiment to the very end, administering what they believed to
be dangerous and severe shocks to the learner-victims. Only five
of the volunteers quit early in the experiment, when the learner-
victims protested the shock treatment. Many of the volunteers
expressed concern for the learner-victim—evidence of their
uncertainty of the propriety of the experiment—and, in some
instances, pleaded with the experimenter to stop the experiment. But in virtually all cases, when the experimenter ordered
them to continue, the participants responded to their ingrained
perception that obedience to the designated authority was their
primary duty and so they obeyed—at a price. In the later stages
of the experiment, many of the volunteers experienced "profuse
sweating, tremor, stuttering and bizarre nervous laughter and
smiling. Three subjects had uncontrollable seizures."[8]

It is a telling feature in the experiment that these people
did not face the dilemma described in the Old Testament
story of Abraham and Isaac, in which Abraham was asked by
his God to sacrifice his only son, Isaac. In the story, God corre-
sponds to the experimenter. Abraham's obedience was
demanded by a respected, trusted, and divine authority—an
excruciating ordeal, but one Abraham faced with trust in the
outcome. In Milgram's experiment, however, the authority figure was a total stranger—not someone who would provoke
feelings of blind trust in the volunteers, especially those whose
age and level of education might have been perceived by them
to be as great or even greater than his. As Laing noted in his
analysis of the experiment, "My guess is that *most* people feel
guilty at *not* doing what they are told, even though they think
it is wrong, and even though they mistrust those who give the
orders. . . . We all have a reflex towards believing and doing
what we are told."[9]

These men believed that when one's conscience is in conflict
with an authority figure, the ethical thing to do is to obey rather

than to trust one's own values and feelings. This rather startling correlation of ethics with obedience is ingrained in most of us, whether we know it or not, and makes it even more difficult for us to work up the courage to defy authority. In most societies, obedience is praised and encouraged primarily for the sake of social stability, predictability, and order, but when obedience is valued per se as an ethically appropriate response, with no consideration given to what is commanded, the result is thoughtless conformity with all its dangerous implications.

Following others in lieu of trusting ourselves is the first non-rational hurdle created by Western culture's way of transmitting ethical values. We learn and advance by transmitting information from one generation to the next, but transmitting values is useful only if individuals critically analyze the values received. The volunteers in Milgram's experiment did not emerge unscathed, and the rest of us must expect similar traumas as we attempt to extricate ourselves from others' authority and assert our own systems. This reflex stunts most people's moral growth and development. If *ethically right* is successfully linked in a person's mind with *obedience to authority,* then a person will avoid independent, critical reasoning, and those perceived to be authority figures in ethical matters will retain an inappropriately strong, or at least undeserved, psychological advantage over their subjects.

Reconciling Authority and Ethical Development

A caveat should be issued before the reader is encouraged to discard all previously acknowledged authorities and, in so doing, end up throwing the baby out with the bath water. Adopting a system of ethical beliefs that is truly one's own does not require abandoning the guidance, advice, and experience of those who have grappled with life's problems and arrived at conclusions we genuinely understand, respect, and would feel comfortable adopting. Ethical maturity broadens the number of acceptable authorities so that no one and nothing is excluded from legitimate consideration, but the ethically mature person will reject those authorities that require unthinking, unquestioning obedience. The justification offered for the atrocities in the Nazi concentration camps, "I was just following orders," is an extreme example of a philosophy that could not have succeeded without blind followers. Ethical maturity ultimately requires accepting responsibility for one's choice of ethical beliefs and for the implications of those beliefs; this level of maturity is achieved through responsible implementation of one's values and modes of behavior. The key to mature ethical behavior recognizes that the norms that are ultimately adopted should comport with the individual's genuine belief structure and general understanding of the world and how the world works. The emphasis is on authentic, wholehearted belief rather than originality.

The question of whether complete ethical maturity is within the grasp of the majority of the population must be considered. Such an accomplishment does, after all, require a level of self-consciousness and intellectual capacity that few people seem to exhibit; by far the greatest number of people rely on someone or something else to tell them what is right and wrong and seem quite content to allow those authorities to fashion for them the details of their everyday lives. The concern is that if word leaks out to the public that people are responsible for their own ethical behavior, there will be pandemonium and all will engage in chaotic and destructive behavior. Such fears, though unrealistic in my opinion, can be addressed and the threat minimized if a small but growing core of independent thinkers gradually introduces somewhat unconventional ideas into the culture. The unrealistic fears arise from misunderstanding how ethical norms and criminal laws motivate us. When we observe the rules of our society, we may be acting out of our ethical beliefs or our fear of prosecution.

Nietzsche, in his condemnations of the herd and the herd mentality, portrayed truly ethical individuals as inevitably outcast, rejected by the rest of the world precisely because their individuality set them apart and therefore threatened those who needed conformity to have security and confidence. Nietzsche described these people as "virtuous," drawing on the Latin *virtus,* meaning "strength," because they exhibited the strength to walk alone and move in their own direction and act on their own approval. Nietzsche's heroes never compromised.

They never seemed to develop the ties with others that create what many more conventional persons would call love and mutual support but that Nietzsche criticized as an ultimate source of unfreedom and weakness.

Nietzsche's heroes bear a striking resemblance to the heroes and heroines of Ayn Rand's novels. They, too, carved their own niches and set their own standards. But although Rand is comfortable allowing her heroes to recognize in each other that unique strength of character and ethical self-sufficiency, she did not continue their development beyond the moment when they decided to join forces as couples to explore the final stage in which individuals retain their integrity but are still able to acknowledge, respect, and complement the uniqueness of others and their ethical systems. We never see the dirty work of compromise and give-and-take that must accompany healthy, ongoing interaction and growth.

The full spectrum of ethical growth ranges from a total reliance on others for rules, approval, and verification of success and progress to a reliance on oneself and one's ability to authentically and freely accept or reject authorities as the individual sees fit. The individual at this latter stage has sufficient security and self-confidence to accept others and their differences without feeling threatened by them or being threatening to them. We are social beings, and an authentic ethical system cannot require total isolation and indifference to others—it must simply rule out unhealthy and destructive dependence on or exploitation of others.

Despite the destructive nature of most people's reliance on others for ethical truths and motivation, rewards, and punishments, it is obvious that such behavior would never survive if it were solely destructive—each of us must have received some benefit for our reliance on others. The commonly acknowledged reward for subscribing to another's set of beliefs is the approval, cooperation, and support of that other. For most of us that other is originally our parents; later it is our friends, our religions, our lovers, and any others we perceive as so valuable to us and our security that we are willing to sacrifice even our autonomy for their approval.

Identifying Stages of Ethical Development

Evaluating one's level of ethical development and prognosis for change and advancement requires, in addition to an assessment of one's intellectual ability and dedication to the project, a realistic view of one's ability to break free of these subconscious, yet incredibly strong, drives. Understanding their strength and ability to dominate even the strongest of us is the first step toward escaping their influence, but mere understanding is not sufficient for the task. Examining one's authorities, adopting a more discerning, open response toward them, and recognizing one's own role as an authority in many ethical matters must take place for us to become fully mature, ethical adults. We each moved naturally enough through the stages when we learned to dress ourselves, first wearing clothes that our parents told us were attractive on us, then wearing clothes that they specifically told us were *not* attractive, and finally developing the confidence to choose for ourselves and respect our own judgment. Independent choices and self-confidence are worthy goals of personal growth and maturation, but unfortunately ethical judgment is not often included in the process. Therefore we are left dependent and perceive ourselves to need an authority to choose for us.

Because these artificial constraints and externally imposed rules direct the ethical development of the individual, the growth process exhibits some unusual features not found in other natural processes. However, the maturation process can be studied and measured and individuals can come to understand their own belief systems in a more objective way once the emotional and intellectual factors have been identified.

Ethical development, like intellectual development, can be tracked through definite stages, and one can estimate one's level of ethical maturity by locating one's present mode of operation along the continuum that plots the intellectual, emotional, and behavioral patterns of the various stages of development. Progression is neither smooth nor predictable nor steadiiy paced for most of us. Just as a child may stall intellectually, for example, in learning to tell time, a person may not readily trust his or her own analysis or question cherished beliefs. Often a person stalls in a stage until a life crisis jolts him or her out of it.

How one's family handles issues of authority and autonomy is a fairly sound indicator of which stages will pose the greatest problems and create the most intense interior struggles as the maturation process unfolds. For example, many people grow up in families in which they are discouraged from trusting their own opinions and abilities to understand and analyze complex problems. They are instead encouraged to look to certain other persons or institutions as superior and trustworthy, regardless of whether such trust and awe are truly warranted. It is difficult for people reared in such an environment to assume responsibility for creating their own ethical systems and to rely on their own gut feelings; the problems and challenges they face stem more from emotional issues than from purely intellectual ones.

William Perry, in his work *Forms of Intellectual and Ethical Development in the College Years,* describes the stages as college students cope with the challenges of foreign, and perhaps radically different, ethical systems and develop their own ethical systems by questioning the values inherited from family, religion, and social background.[10] His scheme, when altered slightly, is also a trustworthy guide to the journey all individuals face as they develop and accept their ethical beliefs. I have revised Perry's scheme slightly and offer the revised version here.

Stage 1: The person sees the world in polar terms of we-right-good versus they-wrong-bad. Right answers for everything are known to an authority whose role is to mediate or teach them.

This mind-set produces the most rigid and dogmatic approach to ethical beliefs. Those who rely on this sort of certainty cling the most tenaciously and desperately to what they believe because they generally have the least security in their position, either because they do not understand the source of their beliefs or because their system has been handed to them with various implicit or explicit threats attached: follow these rules unquestioningly or terrible things—social ostracization, eternal damnation, rejection by family, and so on—will follow. The system becomes more important than the understanding, welfare, or betterment of the subscribers or those around them, but emphasis is placed on rigid obedience to the system rather than on its purpose or the aims it is, or at least originally was, designed to achieve. People caught in this stage are frequently unhappy and uncomfortable with the demands that the system places on them and may not really understand, respect, or even agree with the aims that the system purports to achieve, but that is of little consequence in the face of punishment.

Extreme absolutists will feel compelled to condemn such competing systems, not only for themselves but also for anyone else. People functioning at this stage have no means of distinguishing between the self and others because their system was never presented to them as one that individuals should first understand and then accept or reject based on reasons; reasons were never discussed.

Unfortunately, many religious systems have used this approach to teach ethics. When most people were uneducated and churches educated the public about morals and ethical behavior, the most efficient means of enforcing what the churches considered appropriate behavior was to lay out the rules and then tolerate no disagreement, much as parents do to control their children's behavior regardless of whether the children understand or appreciate the parents' principles. The result, not surprisingly, was a large number of people who accepted the rules and attempted to live by them but who never completely understood why, except for avoiding punishment. As the situations that the rules were to govern changed, the system could not respond or adjust to the new realities. The rules took on a life of their own. The created systems were set on their own rigid paths and were eventually placed outside discussion.

I am reminded of the story of a woman who would always cut a large section from the end of a ham before baking it. When asked by her daughter why, she replied, "I don't really know why; my mother just always did it this way." But her daughter's question aroused her curiosity, so the woman asked her mother, who replied, "Oh, I just always did that because my roasting pan was too small for the large hams I bought!" Cutting off one end of a ham before baking is a trivial behavior, but replicating behavior without understanding the reasons behind it has inflicted great suffering on people when they finally dared to ask "Why?" of authorities who did not know or were afraid to answer. Because we have never experienced a genuinely embraced and appropriate ethical system, most of us will never even think of questioning the reasons behind ethical commands unless, like the woman who cut off the end of the ham, we are fortunate enough to meet someone who prods us and stumble upon a way to fearlessly ask questions and challenge systems we had accepted.

Many people go through their whole lives without challenging the Stage 1 mind-set. They frequently feel the dread, resentment, and insecurity of an adult hemmed in by a system of beliefs that has never been explained and is considered off-limits to intellectual debate. People in this mind-set naturally feel threatened by views that differ substantially from their own precisely because, without a rational basis for belief, they cannot analyze or test competing views: they have no measuring device. The Stage 1 believers can only hope and trust that their system of beliefs is the right one and that all competing systems are wrong. Unfortunately, just as the believers do not know how to judge why their system is right, they are equally ill equipped to understand why the others are wrong.

The first step in moving beyond Stage 1 is to make explicit what one believes, and then to listen to what others with differing views say about their beliefs—not with the intent of winning them over or of abandoning one's own system, but rather with the aim of understanding the issues so that they can be approached as intellectual questions and not merely as rules and regulations.

Stage 2: The person perceives diversity of opinion and uncertainty and accounts for these as confusion engendered by poorly qualified authorities or as exercises designed to encourage individuals to find their own system.

A person moves from Stage 1 to Stage 2 because the ambiguities and the many competing views on ethical matters have become too obvious to deny. The ease and speed of communication with other parts of the globe make isolation and ignorance nearly impossible. When confronted with sufficient disagreement and diversity of beliefs, the Stage 1 believer doubts the sources that explain the ethical system rather than the validity of the system itself. Confusion and disagreement, the Stage 2 believer reasons, signify that the ethical experts have failed to communicate.

This psychological shift is important for two reasons. First, it forces the individual to ask who is responsible for knowing the system and for clearly communicating it to the rest of us. This is the first step toward considering the role of individuals in their quest for a working, reasonable ethical system. Identifying the people or institutions that one holds responsible for such knowledge requires that the individual become conscious of placing trust in others and recognizing their expertise. When one is a child, it is much easier to simply assume that all adults are somehow wise and all-knowing. Compared with us, with our young minds and limited abilities and knowledge, all adults seem consummately competent and aware. But when we become adults, it is difficult to place our trust in the intellectual prowess of a person whose knowledge is limited.

Stage 2 is too early a stage to determine whether the believers will later trust themselves to weigh and decide ethical matters autonomously. But the desire to address diverse ideas rather than to simply deny and ignore or hide from them, (as the Stage 1 believer does) is the first move toward enabling a person to understand and address ethics.

The second reason the step is so significant is that the believer acknowledges that the experts are either (*a*) confused about the ideas themselves or (*b*) inept at communicating them. Stage 2 believers may press for further explanation those authorities that, until now, they obeyed without question. People at this stage begin to think about what is being said and may even experience glimmers of personal insight and awareness, even if in the form of doubt or confusion. They now have a vested interest in understanding their beliefs, because they naively, and probably incorrectly, assume that all disagreement can be resolved and all uncertainty banished.

Stage 2 is a significant step with severe repercussions for most dogmatists because if they continue to seek greater clarity, their beliefs will actually become more murky. Ultimately, if believers pursue the matter long enough, they realize that the experts may not have all the answers. This is a frightening, confusing, and threatening stage. Acknowledging that the problem is more than a mere failure of communication propels Stage 2 believers into Stage 3.

Stage 3: The person accepts diversity and uncertainty as legitimate, but only as temporary conditions in areas for which the authority has not yet found an answer. The perceived uncertainty on the part of the so-called experts makes the person anxious. Therefore, this stage does not last long.

Strong believers find themselves at Stage 3 when key organizations and collectives that dictate beliefs or behaviors make major structural or conceptual shifts. I remember my confusion as a child on being told that although eating meat on Friday was sinful for Catholics a few months ago, before Vatican II's pronouncements, it was not sinful any longer. As a child, I simply responded to the rules as rules—ends in themselves that were to be obeyed—and so changing the rules made no sense and caused me distress. Those who had a better grasp of the purpose of the restriction and of personal sacrifice and penance did not view the shift as I did. They understood the change from imposed penance to voluntary penance. Changing the rule was intended to encourage individual responsibility, but for those who merely followed the rules, the change seemed to threaten the authority of the Church's teachings.

Stage 3 believers have come to accept that the disagreement and uncertainty about ethical beliefs are substantial and that this is not merely the result of poor communication by the authority figures. The believers trust, however, that the disagreement and uncertainty are temporary and that the authority figures will eventually figure out the right answer and achieve a resolution.

This stage is frightening because the believers are straining to trust in the experts while acknowledging that the experts do not, in fact, have any ironclad conclusions to offer. Stage 3 believers experience prolonged stress because they are still ruled by others' views and dictates and are not yet free to explore answers on their own. The believers find themselves at the mercy of the experts as they wait for the right answer and an end to the uncertainty. Because people ultimately must act, with or without ultimate answers, people do not stay at Stage 3 for a long time. When the believers do make choices and take decisive action they can (1) move back to the state of absolute trust and belief (Stage 1), driven by the knowledge that questions lead to uncomfortable gaps and irreconcilable differences (but at least vaguely aware that beliefs are not as settled and secure as they once thought) or (2) move forward by making the first dramatic break with the authorities, reinforced by new confidence in their need for beliefs that are true to their own experience and values.

Stage 4: The person perceives that legitimate uncertainty and diversity of opinion are extensive and concludes that all people have a right to their own opinions. The person rejects ethical authorities in favor of a thoroughgoing relativism in which anyone's opinion, including the individual's, is really as good, true, or reliable as anyone else's.

The shift from Stage 3 to Stage 4 is the most drastic and dramatic shift for the person in his or her development. Like a rubber band that is stretched tightly and then released, the person may experience the move from Stage 3 to Stage 4 as whiplash, as he or she shifts abruptly from too much structure to no structure whatsoever. Stage 4 believers usually make extreme changes in behavior, as they free their habits from the power of the authority figures. They may adopt some changes simply because they perceive them as possible now, regardless of whether they perceive them as beneficial. Most people are overwhelmed by new freedom as they move into this stage.

Stage 4 believers have usually struggled with understandably limited and fallible ethical leaders, and, after clinging and trusting as long as they could, they have accepted that no resolution to the uncertainty and diversity of beliefs dances on the horizon. The grown-ups who seemed so knowledgeable now seem as limited and unsure as the rest of us. Believers are likely to conclude that if there is no real expert and no single, truly right, absolutely perfect answer then why would any answer, including one's own, not be as good as any other? The realization that one might be as right and authoritative as the authorities is intoxicating, and even otherwise very mature persons experience release from the former structures with only the temporary distress one experiences over losing a compass. What comes next is a rush of newfound power and certainty.

The problem, of course, is that people have no idea of how to go about resolving the dilemmas that propelled them through the first three stages; abandoning the old structures does not in and of itself endow people with any new wisdom or plan to guide their new autonomy. Intellectually mature people cautiously consider the old beliefs from the new critical stance, realizing that despite their shortcomings most systems have at least addressed the issues, albeit imperfectly, for years and that there is something to be said for not reinventing the wheel. They want to avoid grabbing the first attractive theory in the panic to settle for some new system; after all, becoming a slave to one's own unconsidered, irrational views and opinions is not a significant improvement over enslavement to another person's or institution's unanalyzed beliefs.

Intellectually immature people taste all the forbidden fruit, staunchly maintaining their right to subscribe to any ethical system they find attractive or easy or profitable. This approach, however, builds one's ethical system on sand because one's tastes, preferences, and needs continually battle to determine one's beliefs, and there is no standard for deciding among them, nothing to turn to as one frantically searches for guidance. To reduce ethical rightness and wrongness to mere matters of personal taste is to destroy the concept of ethics. Why even refer to what is "ethically correct" if all one really means is "preferable at the moment"? For the intellectually mature, preoccupation with newfound freedom eventually subsides and is replaced by the novel experience of struggling for self-determination: if there are no infallible authorities, then what can I believe?

Stage 5: The person perceives all knowledge and values, including those of formerly recognized ethical authorities, as contextual and relativistic and relegates dualistic right-wrong functions to a subordinate status by placing them in context.

Stage 5 represents initial stabilization after the trauma of Stage 4. Although believers still perceive no final answers, absolutes, and infallible authorities, they consider alternative interpretations of key beliefs. In Stage 5, believers begin to see that fallibility and uncertainty need not destroy the notions of right and wrong, good and bad. Perhaps there is no single system of rights and wrongs, but the terms can still be applied in meaningful ways. The terms lose their absolute sense but retain their relative value: perhaps an act cannot be evaluated in the abstract, but once it takes place its ethical correctness can be assessed. This less absolute and less universal use of the terms *right* and *wrong* will seem strange at first to former staunch absolutists who equated these ethical terms with set, universal values, but the ethical system has the same effect on the individual. Ethics provides, after all, a guide for human behavior, and the relativistic sense of right and wrong is, or at least can be, as compelling and binding on the individual as the more universal sense ever was.

The terms *right* and *wrong* do not become meaningless when they become relativized: when individuals acknowledge an act as right or wrong in its context, that acknowledgement has an impact on them and on what they perceive their corresponding duties are. The terms *right* and *wrong* in this sense more closely approximate phrases such as *well fitting* or *poorly fitting* when applied to an overcoat. An overcoat, considered by itself, is neither well fitting nor poorly fitting; those terms gain meaning only when a context is provided. When the coat is tried on a particular individual, the quality of fitting well or poorly becomes concrete and relevant: the coat either fits or it does not. In the same way, an act considered in the context of who and what will be affected and how is either ethically right or wrong, not both and not neither.

If the human mind is the final judge, then, as much as we may hate and resist the idea, we must put aside the longing for an answer that will apply in all situations regardless of the circumstances. We are limited in our knowledge, awareness, and abilities to predict outcomes, so our ethical systems are likewise necessarily flawed. We will at times judge incorrectly and, therefore, act incorrectly, but we hope that by recognizing our fallibility we will resist the urge to badger ourselves and others as we all plod along creating our respective systems. Others' systems appear much less threatening and can even provide a helpful new perspective once the human condition—the great equalizer—is faced once and for all.

Stage 6: The person recognizes that he or she must orient himself or herself in a relativistic world through a personal commitment, as distinct from unquestioned or unconsidered commitment to simple belief in certainty.

Merely recognizing that ethical knowledge is relativistic and lacks universal applicability and certainty does not eliminate one's need for a functioning ethical system. We human beings are ethical beings, regardless of the source we acknowledge as ultimate and authoritative. After the upheaval of clearing away false authorities, individuals need a stable, trustworthy authority and a system that will be reliable, flexible, and, above all, understandable.

In Stage 6 individuals shift from the destructiveness of maturation to the constructiveness of belief formation. They call upon their newfound resources and knowledge as they adopt ethical beliefs that reflect their choices, understanding, and commitment. At first this is an uncomfortable process because all the earmarks of intellectual and emotional security and certainty are missing: the beliefs will be selected, analyzed, and subscribed to according to each individual's say-so and not some outside authority's word or threat. It is surprising to learn how strongly our feelings of certainty are linked with our feelings of trust in the superiority of authorities outside ourselves.

It would be unfair to present this process as one pursued in isolation and in total reliance on one's own intellectual prowess. Each of us naturally seeks out the guidance of those we admire and respect, but the difference between seeking counsel and absorbing another's system is that we understand and choose to accept the other's rules. The rules have a purpose; they are not endowed with a life of their own that will perpetuate the rules beyond their use or applicability. The system remains under the scrutiny of the individual subscribing to it. Commitment is now an intelligent and free act, and placing one's faith in a system of beliefs—without assurance or support or approval of another—is a much more difficult step than all the intellectual groundwork that preceded it. While maturation is primarily a matter of looking over options and adjusting to the demise of old values and norms, believers at this stage still have not committed themselves to the road less traveled. In this step individuals actually buy into the system that they have built, and therefore they make their first positive act of trust in themselves. Letting go of our old ethical authorities, like letting go of much of our reliance on other authority figures as we mature, is painful, but learning to replace those external sources of right and wrong with our own minds and hearts requires adjustment of our intellects and our emotions. Trusting ourselves so completely is not as easy as one might hope.

Stage 7: The person makes an initial, limited commitment.

Constructing one's own genuine ethical system, like constructing our original, externally imposed system, is not accomplished in one sweeping act of commitment: the system does not spring full-blown from one's intellect. As the implications of finitude and autonomy become clear, each individual takes an initial step—a commitment about one issue, in response to a pivotal dilemma, not because it is so profound or so compelling, but rather because it happens to clamor loudest for attention and resolution. The step is a tough one to take because it is the first, tentative step toward intellectual and emotional independence and autonomy. Being willing and able to commit oneself to an ethical belief without the traditional, external motivations, justifications, and rewards or threats is one of the strangest experiences that an adult will ever have. It is as new and challenging as the conceptual shifts that children make as they expand their understanding to see, for example, that not only are they individuals, but they are also members of a group. My mother taught very young children for years and commented to me about a tangible difference between three- and four-year-olds. If she said to a group of three- and four-year-olds, "Let's go outside now," the four-year-olds, who have developed the concept of inclusion in a group, would all go to the door. The three-year-olds, in contrast, would ignore the instruction, because they have not yet developed the concept of group inclusion. Our abilities to form concepts and to understand the implications of our concepts develop in definite steps, and the ability to conceive of oneself as ultimately responsible for one's values and for living according to those values is likewise a giant step in maturation.

Stage 8: The person experiences the initial implications of commitment and explores the subjective issues of responsibility.

Many of us who leave work undone until dangerously close to deadline frequently attempt to justify this foolhardiness by saying "I work better under pressure!" Of course, no one really believes us, but the remark reveals that at times our species responds better to the stick than to the carrot. When we assume responsibility for creating and adhering to our own ethical system, we lose both the carrot and the stick, at least as applied by sources external to us. When I act in ways that I find ethically appropriate and responsible, I earn my own stamp of approval but not necessarily a pat on the back from anyone else. I am responsible to myself for my actions, and that is genuine responsibility, but it does not feel the same as the responsibility I previously had to outside authority figures. As I explore the implications of operating within a system to which I genuinely subscribe, I feel contradictory emotions and will probably have to contend with contradictory signals from those around me. I have met very few people who have successfully progressed to these last few stages, and there are definite reasons for this. Reconciling and standing firm with my approval and others' disapproval of the same action requires a feat of intellectual and emotional gymnastics that challenges the most steadfast believer.

The whole notion of responsibility is experienced at this stage in unfamiliar ways because most of us have accepted the notion that responsibility is always to another. Therefore, having a genuine responsibility to oneself and to one's own freely embraced values may seem to stretch the definition of the term beyond recognition. When we examine how our notions of responsibility and duty were formed, however, we discover that it was in no other person's best interest to encourage us to trust our own judgments about right and wrong. In part, this was a simple matter of authority figures making our behavior conform to what they desired. However, their motives were not merely blatant self-interest or selfishness: these people received their values with the same implicit threats that they used to impart values to us. For us and for them, the process was a relentless exercise in molding, threatening, programming, and, occasionally, rewarding.

Breaking out of this mold and learning to trust one's own ethical ideas occurs gradually and only piecemeal. Typically, individuals encounter a crisis that calls for action but has no plan: they have rejected the old rules and regulations but have not replaced them. They will be forced to make their first commitment to a position. The individuals must learn just how limited or broad their first principle will be as the process unfolds. Nothing will come easily at first. The price of understanding and taking control of one's ethical rule book is the reinforcement and assurance from others that comes from conforming to their standards.

Once the individual acts on the newly embraced rule, the effect will seem unfamiliar. The actors may feel uncertain as to whether they acted correctly or not, because they have not yet formulated a test to indicate whether the actions were really right. In other words, the individual experiences each stage of the process—from agonizing over how to analyze actions and choose rules to looking and longing for assurance that one has, in fact, done well—as new and strange, and, until the individual has repeated the process with several ethical dilemmas, the earmarks of correct thinking and correct acting cannot be known. We have learned to feel comfortable when we have others' approval and uncomfortable when our actions create disapproval in others, at least significant others. What we now must learn, through trial and error, is what it means to experience our own approval and disapproval. Decisions do become easier to make and the results easier to evaluate later, but the fear and uneasiness of this stage are quite real and unavoidable.

One's initial ventures into genuine ethical behavior will bring much uneasiness, uncertainty, discomfort, relentless doubting, and, even after intense soul-searching, probably no clear answer.

Stage 9: The person assumes responsibility for his or her beliefs and realizes that commitment is an ongoing, unfolding activity.

Stage 9 is the ultimate goal; the stage at which individuals have made peace with the changes and uncertainties that arise as they freely choose, form, and adhere to their system of ethical beliefs. They have recognized that the process is fallible and realize that as life and people change, the flexible, responsive system will likewise change. One can make this concession much earlier on the intellectual level, but coming to grips with it at the emotional level requires an ease with the new approach that for most people is slow in coming. To be frank, many of us never achieve it. When we get through blaming our teachers and parents and religious leaders for burdening us with rigid, dogmatic, and unresponsive systems of beliefs, we must acknowledge that we, too, have contributed to the system. Many of us simply want to rely on something solid and certain, and we are so anxious to have closure and certainty that we will gladly accept any ideas, no matter how convoluted or narrow, to settle the questions. So, to abandon the emotional need for absolutes and universals, the individual must achieve the emotional maturity to function as an integrated, knowledgeable, and yet fallible adult and accept the responsibilities of an emotionally mature person. We become more free as we transform ourselves into adults, but with the freedom inevitably comes a heavier responsibility to be aware and connected with our surroundings and the events that affect our relationships with others.

Supporting Maturation in Oneself and Others

Ethical maturation is not an easy process, but achieving self-consciousness, intellectual and emotional freedom, and self-sufficiency is certainly worth the effort. Achieving adulthood in any arena marks a great accomplishment and the realization of the potential that most of us glimpse from time to time but seldom fully realize. Once the goal is recognized as desirable—and worth the effort—and the traps and saboteurs are identified, then what remains is to formulate a plan of action that will provide guidance and support throughout the mission. The process can be supported and encouraged just as effectively as it can be thwarted and frustrated, but the behavior and attitudes required in this effort are, not surprisingly, very different from the behavior and attitudes we observe in society at large.

The monumental step is for all active or aspiring participants in the process to freely discuss possibilities and to consider, in a strictly nonjudgmental manner, the implications of axioms and logical rules. Many of us who sincerely seek understanding and breathing room from others will, nonetheless, respond out of our own narrowness and paranoia when others ask the same of us. If we are truly secure in our own views, we will resist the urge to judge others' views or argue when they attempt to work through their fledgling beliefs through conversation and intellectual exchange. Intellectual freedom requires allowing others the freedom to hold the beliefs they choose and not those I choose, just as I am allowed to hold my chosen beliefs and not theirs. Tolerance is the truly essential virtue because without it no one will be free to ask the initial questions. We cannot expect ourselves or others to jump from a full-blown, overdeveloped system of ethical beliefs into another complete, fully developed system, and bypass the work and real growth we must go through. Very few of us, once past adolescence, would relish the prospect of reliving it, but we acknowledge that we must pass through those developmental stages. The difference here, of course, is that we do not have the comforting companionship of fellow-sufferers and this time we may feel miserable as we wrestle with uncertainty, lack of self-confidence, and the haunting feeling that there is no exit. Society smiles benignly at the angst of the fourteen-year-old, realizing that the suffering will end in a few years, but the adult tackling this process has no timetable and therefore no such ready comfort. For these reasons, the least we should grant ourselves and our fellow searchers is tolerance, patience, and the dignity that comes from self-acceptance and other-acceptance.

Tolerance and patience pertain to the intellectual aspect of maturation, but recognizing human dignity requires a particular emotional stance toward ourselves and others. Our fears of being different will thwart our best efforts if we are not continually on guard. We must resist the urge to bolster our confidence in our own systems by imposing them on our friends and colleagues. If we do, we miss the whole point of allowing each person to adopt the system that is right for him or her.

A woman who read some of Bertrand Russell's works became caught up in the concept of solipsism—the belief that one can be totally certain only of the existence of one's own mind and that others may, in fact, be mere projections of one's subconscious or unconscious or of some other being greater than the individual. The thrust of the doctrine is that for one to be scrupulously honest intellectually, one must be ever on guard to distinguish between what one really knows and what one merely posits, surmises, assumes, or infers. This new disciple of solipsism was so taken with the philosophy that she felt moved to write to Russell to tell him that she was overwhelmed by the obvious correctness and profundity of solipsism; the only thing she could not figure out was why everyone else did not subscribe to it also! Before we are too hard on ourselves for trusting safety in numbers, we should recognize that that axiom has proved its value: our agreement on most beliefs about how the world works has created harmony, cooperation, and loyalty for thousands of years. When we strike out as individuals and create ethical systems that intentionally do not take into account others' support and recognition, we are, most definitely, swimming against the tide that has carried us so forcefully, both individually and as a species, until now.

Acknowledging the dignity of others and the value of their systems does not require that we subscribe to what they say or believe, and recognizing this distinction will mark, for many of us, another innovation in our thinking. For most of us, criticism is the only response we feel comfortable offering when another proposes ideas that differ from our own; in fact, many people seem compelled to jump into a heated argument the moment they sense a different opinion. I have already addressed our natural tendency to project onto our ethical beliefs this objective character that, we are sure, should be universally recognized and appreciated. That tendency may be natural, but it need not be controlling. We can learn to acknowledge without feeling threatened the value of ideas that do not fit our own system but may fit another's system quite well. I acknowledge that person's ethical development and encourage him or her but I do not act or believe as he or she does. I am simply offering to that person the dignity, support, and encouragement that I myself need as I inch my way along the path. In short, we can choose to act as effective catalysts and staunch supports for one another or we can make maturation even more difficult and painful by fueling the fires of self-doubt in ourselves and others and thereby sabotage our own intellectual and emotional liberation and development.

Identifying One's Ethical Beliefs

What Our Cultures Teach Us about Ethics

> What was true for Hank and me holds true for the lion's
> share of ethical impasses among people. They are real, not
> imaginary; yet they are rooted in our imaginations, in the
> way we perceive things, more than in ethical principles or
> rules. They grow out of (1) our differing educational and
> vocational environments; (2) the differing metaphors that
> shape our perceptions of moral issues, and differing images
> of ourselves, of others, of society, of the natural world, and of
> whatever god or center of loyalty provides us with our
> integrity; (3) the differing worldviews or ideologies or myths
> . . . that provide our lives with both setting and standpoint;
> and (4) our differing life experiences. All these differences
> put us in different places in which to be the people we are
> becoming and different vantage points from which to see the
> moral life.[1]

To trace the impact of culturally dictated ethical beliefs by identifying discrete dictates would be to stop one level short of our
desired destination. My culture has not only handed me specific
ethical norms but also has taught me, before I was old enough to
understand ethics, how to think about ethics. The ground must
be cultivated before the ideas can take root. Most people growing
up in the United States in the twentieth century live in a predominantly Judeo-Christian culture strongly related to Western ways
of thinking. These traditions subtly direct our attention to certain

phenomena deemed significant and away from others deemed insignificant or meaningless. The field of ethics is affected necessarily by any development that directs the culture.

To analyze individuals' ethical reasoning apart from their culture is futile. One's ethical stance is largely a consequence of one's relationships, societal advantages or disadvantages, educational opportunities, and career successes or failures. The process builds on everyday experiences and develops as personality and character are formed.

> What inclines us to relate to people in typical ways, to react to certain kinds of people in certain kinds of ways, to tilt toward the interests of a particular group, to focus on particular dimensions of a situation? What makes some people walking humane societies, some portable prosecutors, some touring cleanup squads, and others instant spirit-lifters? What qualities of life will cause people to make good decisions on the many occasions when rights and ideals cannot capture the richness and complexity of the challenge? . . . In addition to focusing on the person faced with ethical choices, our approach calls attention to the fullness of the setting in which the person is interpreting, deciding, and acting. Our surroundings include both the values in the air and the ones in our blood.[2]

The twentieth century is obsessed with science because that endeavor has overcome nature and nearly banished uncertainty from our future. We assume, mistakenly, that science must be the answer to all our questions and needs. However, when scientists began scrutinizing our species in the hope of neatly classifying and explaining our nature, they overlooked a conflict of interest. To study human nature objectifies it and declares it something capable of isolation, study, and, most importantly, accurate prediction. To make something an object of study presumes that it behaves regularly and that it obeys certain laws that themselves can be identified, learned, and then applied successfully. The term *social science* connotes an exact study, with methods similar to those used in the physical sciences, but applied to human beings, social animals. The practitioners claim they can reduce human nature and human behavior to a domain of the physical world of cause and effect. Our faith that full understanding and predictability of human behavior is waiting for the right scientist to discover it is a culturally created and transmitted bias that strongly shapes our dispositions toward ethical beliefs. Tugging against this bias is our sense that we enjoy a fundamental freedom when we act and that freedom, to be genuine, would have to resist the regularity and predictability that science presumes.

If we truly believe that our behavior is as mechanical as the boiling of water, then this belief will act as a subconscious filter and we will interpret the world accordingly. Our expectations of ourselves and others reflect our biases, and, inevitably, we take as facts mere cultural beliefs or theories, as though we believe mass acceptance provides additional proof and creates an aura of infallibility around these theories. Our filters push us toward pessimism or optimism about our fellow human beings and our universe.

Consider the following hypothesis, offered by social scientist Alfie Kohn to address the cultural imposition of beliefs about human nature and potential and the power of those beliefs.

> In order to rationalize the blizzard of cruelty and aggression in contemporary society, it is helpful, and occasionally therapeutic, to believe that it is not always possible to control open anger, rivalry, and jealousy. This rationalization mutes feelings of guilt and dilutes a continuing sense of personal responsibility for hurting others. The Japanese, by contrast, believe that each person can control his or her anger, and the differential frequency of violence in Tokyo and New York implies that if people believe they can tame their aggressive impulses they often do.[3]

Kohn tackles the pessimism he perceives in our culture's view of human nature and asks the obvious question: Considering the damage to our self-esteem and our esteem for others caused by our culture's view of human nature, why would such a bias ever take root? Whose interests are served by this destructive practice? Kohn concludes that the theory that we ultimately cannot be responsible or in control offers everyone an unassailable excuse for both laziness and gross irresponsibility, so all of us benefit from such a theory. If all our actions are merely mechanical manifestations of physical impulses and processes that we cannot effectively manage, then we are all let off the hook: parents really have no control over their children, therefore they cannot fail them; teachers have no genuinely effective influence on their charges; and none of us is really responsible for how we treat one another, whether in our families or the larger community. We simply assert that there is no real responsibility in the world, and then we internalize the belief that we not only cannot control others effectively, we really cannot control even ourselves. We become rich scientific subjects but ignoble people. We turn away from ourselves when we ask how to improve the condition of human life and look instead to the scientists to program us better or to more quickly identify the gene responsible for crime, prejudice, and selfishness and eliminate it. It seems that we regularly cite examples of human failure and wretchedness in our newspapers to reinforce the idea that, surely, if we could alleviate this suffering, we would have done so by now. The existence of so much bad in the world is overwhelming and seems to convince us that we must be powerless. Convincing ourselves, holding out this hypothesis as a bona fide fact, reinforces the power of such strongly grasped and nurtured beliefs.

That our beliefs add to the texture of the reality around us complicates ethical issues and blunts the hard edges of scientific facts and scientific method. Unlike the boiling point of water, over which one's emotions and preferences exert no control, the moment when one abandons hope in one's fellows is affected by one's social relationships. Significant facts in the social sciences are susceptible to my influence. Our beliefs, coupled with the actions that they dictate, alter the quality of life around us. As William James pointed out at the turn of the century, our belief that a particular value is or is not worth holding can tip the scale in favor of its verification or falsification, at least to the extent that we experience the value and therefore to the extent that we attribute weight to it in our minds.

Every human being must sometime decide for himself whether life is worth living. Suppose that in looking at the world and seeing how full of misery, of old age, of wickedness and pain, and how unsafe is his own future, he yields to the pessimistic conclusion, cultivates disgust and dread, ceases striving, and finally commits suicide. He thus adds to the mass *M* of mundane phenomena, independent of his subjectivity, the subjective complement *x*, which makes of the whole an utterly black picture illumined by no gleam of good. Pessimism completed, verified by his moral reaction and the deed in which this ends, is true beyond a doubt. *M+x* expresses a state of things totally bad. The man's belief supplied all that was lacking to make it so, and now that it is made so the belief was right.[4]

Our awareness that our very act of believing and our subsequent action on that belief can alter realities—the outcomes of events—creates a new responsibility for the mature, ethical individual. I have a genuine duty to learn what I can and believe properly because my errors contribute, in a very concrete way, to perpetuating the errors and misconceptions that drive others to act unwisely or unethically in the face of ignorance and misplaced beliefs.

This awareness is particularly pertinent to the realm of ethics because, for some questions of value, belief itself becomes a necessary component of the belief's verification. We play an active role in making a belief true or false and how we act will guarantee whether a belief turns out to be true or false.

Suppose, for example, that I am climbing in the Alps, and have had the ill-luck to work myself into a position from which the only escape is by a terrible leap. Being without similar experience, I have no evidence of my ability to perform it successfully; but hope and confidence in myself make me sure I shall not miss my aim, and nerve my feet to execute what without those subjective emotions would perhaps have been impossible. But suppose that, on the contrary, the emotions of fear and mistrust preponderate; or suppose that, having just read the Ethics of Belief, I feel that it would be sinful to act upon an assumption unverified by previous experience,—why, then I shall hesitate so long that at last, exhausted and trembling, and launching myself in a moment of despair, I miss my foothold and roll into the abyss. In this case (and it is one of an immense class) the part of wisdom clearly is to believe what one desires; for the belief is one of the indispensable preliminary conditions of the realization of its object. *There are then cases where faith creates its own verification.* Believe, and you shall be right, for you shall save yourself; doubt, and you shall again be right, for you shall perish. The only difference is that to believe is greatly to your advantage.[5]

An old "M*A*S*H" episode on television dealt with the common problem in wartime of many casualties and not enough medical supplies. The surgical unit had several seriously injured soldiers who had undergone surgery and were suffering tremendous pain. A shipment of morphine was waylaid by black marketeers. The doctors were concerned that some patients might die. The older doctor, the head of the unit, decided to distribute placebos to the patients and tell them they were receiving morphine. The younger doctors were skeptical about both the ethics and the effectiveness of such an action, but they finally decided to distribute the fake pills. The patients took the medicine believing that it would relive their pain. Soon all but one patient reported great relief from the pain and were able to rest comfortably. The older doctor told the one who felt no relief that the medicine was, of course, very strong but that he felt a man of his great physical strength could probably tolerate two pills, and so doubled the soldier's dose. The second placebo did the trick. This soldier too was able to rest and recover.

This phenomenon is not foolproof, but each of us has, at one time or another, fooled ourselves into accepting some dubious belief and thereby avoided pain, disappointment, or disillusionment. But the power to override incredibly stubborn and strong objective realities is, nonetheless, a double-edged sword: self-deception and denial are, for some, easy ways to avoid difficult realities. Intellectual honesty is one's only protection against not only error from without, but also from within.

Our impressions and beliefs wield great power over our perceived realities. Therefore we should no doubt be much more concerned about passively absorbing the data that bombard us from all sides. We should be more selective about what we accept as fact. That certain values and impressions come to us via our 1990s American culture lends them an air of credibility that should be regarded with great skepticism. For example, I could easily draw some bizarre conclusions about life in America if I believed MTV accurately reflects how most or all people in the United States think and feel. Continual bombardment by an idea wears down my resistance to it, and I find that, at times, an idea has crept into my worldview quite insidiously despite my efforts to resist it and think independently. When I often hear of child abuse and domestic violence, what do I believe about family relationships? What do I consider the norm? Do I accept as virtually inevitable the notion that people really do not care about each other, do not respect each other, and cannot act in a civilized manner toward one another? How do these conclusions influence my beliefs about the ethical quality of these actions?

Kohn points out our pejorative use of the words *human* and *human nature,* in instances when we say "Oh, well, I'm only human" as an excuse for both forgetfulness and gross stupidity.[6] We impute to human nature our selfishness, our fierce competitiveness, and our other frailties. We call on our human nature to rationalize our weaknesses and failings, but when speaking of our accomplishments we never say, "Oh, well, it was just human nature." We seem to really think, or at least our language certainly indicates, that when we fail, it is because of our flawed natures but that when we succeed, it demonstrates some superior virtue or intellect and we gladly accept praise and credit. We, of course, want it both ways: to be cleared of responsibility when we fail and to be fully responsible when we succeed. Kohn wants to temper both those extreme tendencies and to acknowledge more responsibility for our failures and a little less for our successes. He attempts to defuse the pervasive cultural belief that humans are by nature selfish and competitive. He points out that even Adam Smith, whose hallmark was his preoccupation with the self-interest principle, commented about our other drives:

How selfish soever man may be supposed, there are evidently some principles in his nature, which interest him
in the fortune of others, and render their happiness necessary to him, though he derives nothing from it, except
the pleasure of seeing it. . . . That we often derive sorrow
from the sorrow of others, is matter of fact too obvious to
require any instances to prove it.[7]

A study Morton Hunt described in *The Compassionate Beast*
traced the development of altruistic tendencies in human subjects ranging from newborns to high school seniors.[8] Hunt
aimed to observe whether our altruistic tendencies go
through the same developmental stages as other human characteristics, such as the ability to perceive and recognize spatial
qualities. Hunt hoped that, if altruistic tendencies naturally
developed along with self-oriented tendencies, he could give
our assessment of humankind greater balance and optimism.
He observed that newborns cry when they heard other infants
cry, but he interpreted their behavior as a response to their
own discomfort rather than a response to another child. At
this stage, their discomfort was primarily a selfish response,
not an expression of concern for others. About the age of ten
to fourteen months, the young children responded more
overtly to another's distress: they stared tensely and whim-
pered, cried, or ran away. They still showed no inclination to
help the other person, but they did seem to be discomforted
by the discomfort of another. Although they may have been
selfishly motivated, they did show some empathy. At age fif-
teen months and older, the children made greater efforts to
help, patting or stroking the distressed person or, occasionally,
hugging or kissing that person. Children over eighteen
months old were more direct: they would attempt to alert an
adult, or they would bring the distressed person objects that
they found comforting and reassuring, such as a toy, a cookie,
or a baby bottle. All the children's actions reflected their level
of development, their communication skills, and their general
level of social interaction.

If this study is accurate, then concern for others is as natural
as distrust or competitiveness: we are truly social animals, and
we are drawn to interaction with those around us in both selfish

and unselfish ways. We develop not only a set of selfish and competitive qualities, but also a repertoire of caring and cooperative ones. Accenting the first set as the more basic, more real responses, orients us to expect a cruel, uncaring world and prepares us to approach others warily, not readily trusting others and always on guard against others' ulterior motives.

For example, we may give the worst possible interpretation to others' words and actions. A man drove up a steep, winding road that was so narrow that only a single car could easily pass. Where the road was most treacherous, he stopped for a moment to rest and got out to stand beside his car. A second car that was descending along the same road came around a sharp bend toward him and, as it passed, the female driver leaned out and yelled, "Pig!" The man shook his fist at the vanishing figure and yelled, "Sow!" He climbed back into his car, drove up the mountain and, as he made the sharp turn, he hit a pig.

I was told by a friend from Texas, who was interested in the history of that state, about a tribe of Native Americans whose culture was greatly at odds with the culture that was being forced on them as Europeans settled in the wild West. This very proud people apparently realized that assimilation into the white settlers' culture was out of the question: they might be able to survive as a group, but certainly their culture would not. They decided as a group to sterilize themselves by eating a wild plant. They moved about as nomads, staying far enough ahead of the white settlers to avoid annihilation, while living out the last years of their tribe's existence according to their values and ways and anticipating their extinction. According to the story, the tribe did not cite any particular ethical beliefs to explain their choice, and yet their decision and action reflect definite, discernible ethical notions. As a group, they were convinced that death is preferable to life without their culture. Freedom to live as one feels one should or as one cares to is a need our species feels deeply. Many view freedom as more essential to one's personhood than life itself. The people's profound commitment revealed much of what they took to be essential for a good life, a life worth living. How they chose to express that commitment—in electing to move on and avoid violence rather than confront the foe and die in battle—likewise said much about their view of how peoples should relate. That one comes away from the story with a sense of this people's pride, integrity, and strongly ethical motives indicates that one need not read a group's moral treatises to grasp their ethical beliefs.

Revelations about a society's ethics are found in unexpected places. For example, among Harriet Martineau's contributions to sociological methodology is an observation about the most efficacious means of identifying a culture's ethical beliefs. She notes that the most obvious tack would seem to be to ask someone, perhaps even several members of the group, and then simply record the group's responses. But, she notes, people within the same culture will tell you of many diverse, even contradictory, ethical dictates and if you persist in polling more and more persons with the hope of uncovering a pattern, you will most likely become thoroughly confused and farther from their beliefs.

> To arrive at the facts of the condition of a people through the discourse of individuals is a hopeless enterprise. The plain truth is—it is beginning at the wrong end. The grand secret of wise inquiry into Morals and Manners is to begin with the study of THINGS, using the DISCOURSE OF PERSONS as a commentary upon them.
>
> Though the facts sought . . . relate to Persons, they may most readily be learned from Things. The eloquence of Institutions and Records, in which the action of the nation is embodied and perpetuated, is more comprehensive and more faithful than that of any variety of individual voices. The voice of a whole people goes up in the silent workings of an institution; the condition of the masses is reflected from the surface of a record. The Institutions of a nation—political, religious or social—put evidence into the observer's hands as to its capabilities and wants, which the study of individuals could not yield in the course of a lifetime. The records of any society, be they what they may, whether architectural remains, epitaphs, civic registers, national music, or any other of the thousand manifestations of the common mind which may be found among every people, afford more information on Morals in a day than converse with individuals in a year.[9]

The institutions she mentions are, for the most part, outside most citizens' consciousness. For example, a convention that she singles out as particularly revealing is setting a particular event as the origin of time for the society. What are the landmark dates of a culture? What events does each culture single out as worthy of special status in the mind of every person? It reveals much to us to realize that Western cultures count their years from the birth of Christ, while other cultures use other dates as reference points. In the United States, for example, every schoolchild can recite the significance of 1492, 1776, and 1941.

That the landmark dates almost always relate to wars or treaties or revolutions also reveals much about a people's notions of what is significant. As Martineau points out, we would experience a revelation and a jolt to our systematized morality if we happened upon a civilization that separated its epochs by salient dates in the history of art, literature, philosophy, or even science. What does it say about our notion of history that we treat it predominantly as a progression of political events rather than, say, cultural ones? What might it require for a society to view its history in terms of its great advancements in medicine or perhaps its greatest works of art? Our choices tell us about what we consider important, and that always reveals something about a society's ethical sensitivity, whether the picture is flattering or not.

Another institution that readily reveals a people's ethical axioms is its legal system, or, as in the case of the United States, two systems: common law and the civil law based on the Napoleonic Code (which is the basis for the legal system in only one state, Louisiana). The orientations of the two systems reflect their contrasting views of human nature. Common law is created through precedent—how the courts have interpreted and applied legal concepts. Common law views the law as essentially negative in nature: it sets out the minimum that a person must do to stay out of trouble. If one drops below the standard set by law, one becomes liable to one's fellow citizens under the law. The Napoleonic Code, on the other hand, does not, at least theoretically, build on precedent; it always advises one to return to the code to consider the original dictum. It distrusts precedent because the original dicta do not set out the minimum behavior that is acceptable, but rather set out what the ideal behavior would be. Under this system, we are not interested in how the court interpreted the rule in a particular case. We are concerned, rather, with considering what the best behavior would have been, and then determining how this behavior measures up to that standard.

Each society's moralities, needs, and notion of human nature are different, and under the Napoleonic Code their laws would differ accordingly. For example, the legal systems of most European countries that are based on the the Napoleonic Code include Bad Samaritan statutes, laws dictating that one has an affirmative duty to help those who are in life-threatening situations. So, if I were sitting by a swimming pool and a small child (no relation of mine) were to toddle over to the edge and fall in, then, under the Bad Samaritan statutes, I would be obliged to at least toss in the life preserver or, perhaps, even reach over to help the child, assuming that would not jeopardize my life and health. Under common law I would have no legal obligation at all. I can sit idly by and watch the child drown. I may be judged ethically bankrupt and a disgrace to the human race, but I cannot be charged with a crime because under common law as long as I do nothing to actively hurt you, I have not exhibited the selfish, destructive behavior that we term a *crime.* Again, the emphasis is on the negative function of the law and on pinpointing the minimum obligation owed to another. Although many of us would prefer that our fellow citizens help us if we were drowning, our society has never successfully incorporated legal requirements to perform altruistic actions. However, in those systems in which laws set out what would be ideal human behavior, creation of affirmative obligations makes sense because the law is seen as a positive guide, concerned with prescribing the best human behavior. Law then functions to improve human relations, encourage behavior that is more ethical, and so on. Each society's implicit beliefs about how its citizens are motivated, how they can and should act toward one another, and what they should value as significant cultural achievements are the moral criteria for what is socially acceptable behavior. The legal codes that actually articulate the society's ethical norms are almost anticlimactic.

Another institution that Martineau considers pivotal in revealing a society's ethical beliefs is its penal system—its methods for dealing with criminals. She treats the history of the correctional system of a society as almost a mini-history of its ethical progress. More primitive means of treating criminals indicate an ethical insensitivity to those outside the privileged classes. More pronounced moves to rehabilitate, rather than merely punish, indicate an a tempering of the natural impulse to retaliate when harmed, and therefore represent a more mature ethical attitude toward those who harm society. There need not be explicit documentation of a society's ethical position on dealing with criminal behavior for one to understand it; behavior alone is the key, and behavior is also the surest indicator of what has been internalized, as opposed to merely expressed.

The movie *A Clockwork Orange* painted an intriguing picture of a fictional society's approach to rehabilitation. A major character in the film was convicted of rape and murder and was brainwashed to destroy his ability to act on violent impulses. As a result of this conditioning, he suffered severe and debilitating sickness whenever he felt an urge to do violence. This solution enabled him to remain in society, permanently rid of the ability to repeat his crime. Therefore, the rehabilitation worked in that it cured the patient, but at the cost of his autonomy. Because our culture values personal freedom and autonomy, we consider the film's solution to the problem unacceptably degrading and dehumanizing, and yet our culture does not consider life imprisonment destructive of the human essence. Where each culture draws the line reveals that culture's ethical position on which characteristics of personhood are too sacred to be compromised.

Numerous other institutions are likewise instructive: consider the themes and subject matter of a culture's most popular movies, books, and magazines; its regard for the education of its youth; its support services for its families; its treatment of the mentally ill. Of course, consideration of all of these institutions and activities will yield valid results only if it

is conducted with a balanced perspective, neither overly pessimistic nor blissfully ignorant of the hard realities that also
form the picture. Ethical beliefs show themselves in action,
and the major institutions that support the social system
provide us with continual opportunities to put our ethics
into action.

The social institution that probably steers a society's ethical
progress most overtly is, of course, a society's religions.
Religious organizations have always served as the main teachers and preservers of codified ethical belief systems within
every society. The more diverse the society, the more permuta-
tions of the belief systems one finds. Traditions and rituals are
handed down from one generation to the next to keep the
religion pure and in harmony with its original "charter," but
many acquire subtle alterations over the generations. In some
cases, the conditions that prompted a certain regulation or
command no longer prevail or threaten the society. In others,
the meaning of the ritual or rule may be misconstrued or
entirely forgotten. For a religion to maintain its credibility, it
must maintain ties with its source or founder. Among
Christian religions, for example, a sect must be able to trace its
line of authorities back to Jesus Christ and his apostles because
Christ himself is the pivotal authority figure.

Religion provides a framework in which believers can place
their individual lives and actions and interpret their meaning
and purpose. This framework includes its own ethical stance
toward the world by stipulating what constitutes a life well lived.
The dominant religions gradually impose many of their more
important assumptions on the society by influencing large numbers of people. Despite extensive doctrinal differences among
the various Christian sects, for example, all embrace the values
spoken by Christ in the Beatitudes. The particulars may differ,
but a Christian orientation toward life includes some very broad
features: love as the supreme virtue; faith in a caring, personal
God; and emphasis on an afterlife as the destiny of humankind.
These features provide a rudimentary ethical system, with only
the details to be worked out by the individual. The existing religious structures may prove useful for those forming their own
systems, but their existence sometimes makes individuals forget

to question the familiar (since the familiar feels right, even when it lacks intellectual justification) and can hamper the individual's spiritual development. The influence exerted by the stronger, more established religious sects is even greater than their proponents imagine, and it reaches far beyond formal doctrines, affecting some of the most improbable features of a culture's secular institutions. Consider, for example, the following imprints that Christianity has made on Western culture: Santa Claus; our linear notion of time; our calendar, using B.C. and A.D. as markers; even our twelve-member juries, reflecting the selection of the Twelve Apostles.

However, the impact of religion on its followers' ethical views is more than leading them to accept a list of specific beliefs or dogmas. Religion provides a rich and pervasive context that provides a way of seeing the world and the individual's place in it. In this respect religions function like myths, as Hunt writes:

> Myths give us our bearings, and they filter our perceptions overwhelmingly. Our myths underlie our morals, and we absorb them with the air we breathe rather than select them after a survey of options. Religion is basically mythic, and people who grow up in a particular religious setting will always carry the imprint of that ambiance even though they may reject that religion and give their allegiance to some other worldview.[10]

The Inevitable Overlap between Religious and Cultural Worldviews

One need not profess belief in or practice a particular religion or faith to find religious overtones in one's worldview. Every culture's ethical system incorporates at least some religious values. Who within our own culture has never articulated the golden rule? Why does "In God We Trust" appear on our currency? Of course, the words alone do not make us all religious believers, much less a people trusting in God, but our experience of our religions and our cultures is intertwined, and, because neither is a totally static institution, each colors the other and provides both support and tension as the two attempt to survive and grow, not so much side by side, but rather as separate organs within the same organism.

The doctrines within Western religious systems reveal much about why they have dominated Western ethical systems and why they have generally discouraged individuals from independently evaluating traditional ethical beliefs. Western religions share a belief in a personal God who created humans for a purpose. Furthermore, this God loves his (until recently Western religions treated God as a necessarily masculine being) creatures and desires for all to live as he intended them to live and to join him for eternal reward at the end of this life. Because attaining this reward depends on discerning God's will and following it, much emphasis is placed on revelation and on faith and good works. God is a personal being who set the universe into motion and who foresees its end. In the history of Western religious thought a debate rages over how humans can be free and responsible if God already knows, and knew before the creation of the species, what every human being would do during his or her life. How the debate is resolved is critical for the believer who faces any significant ethical dilemma. For those sects that believe in predestination, the answer is, at least for the elect, a huge relief: the elect were chosen by God ahead of time and therefore are already destined for their heavenly reward. Those who are less fortunate, of course, feel mistreated but are reminded that because we are all sinners no one deserves eternal reward, and so the elect are escaping their just reward, damnation.

Those sects that cannot reconcile human freedom with divine foreknowledge are required to redefine their terms—particularly the term *omniscience*—in order to escape the paradox. If we truly are free, then there must have been a genuine possibility that, at any moment, I might have done something other than what I decided to do. Perhaps God knows all the possibilities that I faced and may even, as a good friend might, be able to predict what I would most likely do, but if I am genuinely free, then the event cannot have been set before my birth. Christianity has endeavored to decipher the meaning of human existence, and has built up a tremendous superstructure of doctrines, dogma, and, of course, ethical rules.

A Western Christian bias is so much a part of our thinking that we have become desensitized to it, but a comparison of Western religious views (which dominate our culture) and Eastern religious views reveals some of the more subtle influences that have infiltrated even our most secular institutions. Consider, for example, our Western belief that time is linear in nature. This notion would strike most people as totally nonreligious and simply common-sensical, and yet in the Eastern worldview and in most Eastern religions time is viewed as a cyclical process. Our Western notion comes from the traditional religious explanation of the origins of the universe: that God created his universe according to his plan and set it in motion, and now the plan will be played out until the end of the universe, which may be directly signaled by an act of God or may be indirectly willed by God through his creatures, easily accomplished these days with nuclear weapons. (We retain in our legal terminology the phrase *act of God* to describe those conditions that cannot be diverted, warded off, or avoided by human effort.) We represent time as a straight line, along which we chart the unfolding of the divine plan, not according to human values or goals, but according to divine ones. Our image of ourselves as links in the chain of humankind expresses the same theme. Students who have grown up with the Western bias and study Eastern religions often find the treatment of human actions and destiny to be overly impersonal and the notion that time more closely resembles a spiral than a straight line to be unsettling, although—from a simply common-sensical point of view—we experience time in cycles such as the seasons, the generations, and rebirth in nature. The religiously based Western worldview dictates that we have individuated egos that are not simply reabsorbed into the cosmos upon our demise, and even if we consciously discard Western religious beliefs and declare ourselves atheistic or agnostic, we nonetheless treat the self as an egotistical, individuated agent and time as an eternal straight line. We do not escape the impact of religion by declaring ourselves outside its domain: it infiltrates the most seemingly secular aspects of our lives and leaves an indelible mark on our thinking.

Understanding the Transmission Process

In *The Compassionate Beast,* Hunt includes a chapter entitled "The Making of Altruists," in which he addresses the factors that affect the development of altruistic tendencies in the individual, factors that lie outside the control and usually awareness of that individual.

The major factors that Hunt lists include the parent-child relationship, modeling, discipline and training, labeling, learning by doing, social interaction, and sexual roles.[11] In addition to these strongly influential socializing experiences that affect us primarily in our youth, he also addresses additional factors that seem to affect adult behavior and direct our interests and impulses either toward or away from altruistic behavior. Hunt's commitment to the proposition that imposing rules and punishments is ineffective in creating a genuinely altruistic attitude reinforces the claim that externally imposed ethical systems may, in the long run, cause more harm than good. Genuine ethical goodness is more than merely mimicking others' behavior or following others' rules; standards must be internalized and experienced as commensurate with one's deepest beliefs and most profound understanding of the world. There comes that moment, inevitably, when every thinking person needs to understand why life should be lived this way and no other, and when an adult understandably balks at being told that this is just how life is or that the rules are somehow more important than a person's feelings, thoughts, and experiences: our experiences do count, must count in our analysis of the meaning of the good life.

Parent-Child Relationships

The nature of one's relationship with one's parents affects how one forms ethical beliefs substantially because we absorb many of our axioms from our parents. How trusting we are, how threatening or nurturing we find the world are tied securely to how our parents have responded to us and to the world, or at least as we perceived them to respond. Ethical behavior, like altruism, requires us to care for and reach out to others, and this requires more security and stability than, unfortunately, many homes provide. Parents are our first source of care and support, and it is essential to each person's ethical development that in those first years, when we are weak and vulnerable, our parents treat us lovingly and fairly. If they do not respond to us in ethically sound and sensitive ways, then we will not readily learn such behavior or practice it toward others. Parents are not, of course, perfect and cannot be expected to always act in an ideal manner, but we must have a sense of trust and trustworthiness, reliability, and fairness in them if we are to develop ethical sensitivity and concern for others. If one is very lucky, one's supporting community (extended family, neighborhood, church, and so on) can compensate for the deficiencies of our parents, but many people do not have these other social supports.

Unfortunately, many parents believe their influence over their children's ethical development is limited to the rules and regulations that they articulate as opposed to the way they live. The mountain of popular psychology books on adult children of alcoholics, transgenerational disorders, codependency, and other problems stemming from dysfunctional family relationships should help educate parents about the pervasive impact of family relationships. If parents wield sufficient power to strengthen or warp our self-esteem, cripple us in our adult relationships, and sabotage our successes in personal and professional arenas, we should expect them to seriously affect the early development of our ethical selves.

Modeling

Modeling is probably the most powerful means of shaping our behavior as young children. We copy what we see our parents do and internalize their roles, social functions, and so on as the standards for behavior, since we have no other standards with which to compare them. And even if we come to see that their behavior was grossly inappropriate, we will experience substantial emotional obstacles to revising those internalized patterns and roles. Our species learns all of its practical functions by modeling; we copy long before we can consciously evaluate the appropriateness of what we are copying. A colleague told me that he and his father were walking through a city in the dead of winter and came upon a homeless man, shivering in the cold wind. My friend said that his father took off his own coat and gave it to the man, explaining to the young son that he had other coats at home but that this man had nothing else. The incident quite naturally made a deep impression on my friend and taught him an invaluable lesson about caring for others; the naturalness and spontaneity of his father's generosity taught a more profound lesson about charity and caring than a hundred treatises could.

The modeling my friend observed was, of course, of the positive variety; it enriched his life and his bond to others. But, unfortunately, in our society, a wide array of negative behaviors is also demonstrated by parents who do not even suspect that they are contaminating their children's views of life and damaging their self-esteem. I recently observed two women in their thirties having lunch in a nice restaurant. Each had brought along one child. The children, both girls, were about three years old. One of the women did nothing but complain through the entire meal about how poor the service was, how bad the weather was, how inferior the stores' merchandise was these days, and so on. Likewise, her daughter whined throughout the entire lunch, alternating between noisy, incessant clamoring for attention and subdued pouting punctuated by occasional emotional outbursts. The other woman spent the entire time nodding sympathetically, making consoling gestures and offering emotional support. Her daughter never uttered a word either, but spent the entire time watching the pouting child rant and rave and, when the child seemed on the verge of a tantrum, even offered her own cookies and her own toy to the other child. If the scene had not been so pathetic it would have appeared ludicrous and silly, but, in fact, I was witnessing exactly how parents can poison their children's outlooks on the world by providing strongly negative modeling and demonstrating poor coping skills. How our parents perceive the world and social relationships is the bulk of our experience with coping skills in our earliest years. If they respond to the world as though it is threatening, beyond their control, and unpredictable, then we learn that our actions count for very little in the larger sphere, and the search for a secure little niche can thrust all other concerns into the background.

Modeling is not restricted to our childhood. Because of my upbringing in a small town, I repeat behaviors in Chicago that are clearly not typical in the big city, although they were, and still are, perfectly appropriate in a small town. For example, I almost invariably say "thank you" to the bus driver as I exit the bus. If I exit the bus first and those behind me hear me thank the driver, very often one or two people behind me will, likewise, thank the driver. However, if I exit last, I almost never hear a "thank you" from anyone. I have noticed this so frequently and consistently that I am convinced that those people behind me who extend themselves to the driver do so because they have just heard me do that. We imitate others every day—sometimes we suffer from and then spread another's bad mood or, if we think of it, we can act to defuse that person's bad mood and create a more positive feeling in them and others. Modeling is not necessarily a sure thing: sometimes I may say "thank you" and no one else will, but a useful method need not work 100 percent of the time. It is sufficient to know that I can make an impact, at least from time to time, simply through my own example.

Discipline and Training

Discipline and training, by far the most widely used means of instilling ethical norms, are, according to Hunt, probably also the least effective. This method can be observed everyday on playgrounds across the United States as parents and teachers attempt to create unselfish children by scolding them when they act selfishly and then insisting that they engage in some unselfish act, such as sharing a favorite toy or taking turns on a favorite ride. The desired effect is that the child internalizes the norm and then, next time, spontaneously acts according to the norm. Hunt found, however, that discipline and training can effectively change short-term behavior but seems to have little impact on long-term attitudes. The children will comply—begrudgingly, resentfully, angrily—but will not incorporate unselfish behavior into their own repertoire of actions. If the goal is to instill the value behind the behavior, the value will be discarded as the children struggle to break free from the externally imposed restraints.

Labeling

The impact of labeling is of great current interest as our society struggles to contain the dramatic rise of juvenile violent crime. Juvenile courts now take labeling so seriously that they deliberately use terminology that is much more neutral and has a less harsh connotation than that used in the adult criminal system. The mere act of labeling juveniles "delinquent," for example, reduces their chances of correcting their behavior and reforming themselves because the internalized stigma reinforces the bad behavior.

Formerly, it was believed that if a person were labeled in a negative way by society, the person would be shocked and dismayed by the label and decide to break free of that image, thereby earning a better label from the society. However, labeling seems to create the opposite effect: instead of working against the label, the person seems to accept what the label says about him or her. The label becomes a self-fulfilling prophecy and defeats its own purpose. Of course, positive labeling would, likewise, encourage more positive behavior, just as the negative labeling fueled negative responses. Hunt found that children who were praised for helping others and were specifically told that they had shared and that they were children who liked to help others were more likely to respond again in altruistic ways, while youngsters who were praised for sharing but were not described explicitly as those who liked to help others but instead were merely told that they had acted as they were expected to act were less likely to respond again in altruistic ways. All the stress on positive reinforcement seems to have been appropriately placed, if Hunt's findings are correct, because it would indicate that if we want people to become more ethical and more altruistic we should do less scolding and more reinforcing. Telling people that they are people of strong ethical character or great integrity can help them become precisely that.

Learning by Doing

Under learning by doing, Hunt discusses how values are learned when one conducts oneself in an ethical or altruistic manner and then experiences a positive effect. Taking part in the process, seeing the results of kind, thoughtful, ethical treatment of others is, as the adage goes, its own reward. Learning by doing requires that we do more than merely tell others, especially our children, about how to act ethically or just set out the rules. If we want to help transmit the ethical values in the society, then we must seek out opportunities for learners to practice those values and experience the positive results of their actions.

Social Interaction

Social interaction supplies the strongest stimulus for ethical action: a bonding with and an appreciation of others who are very different from oneself. Ethical behavior frequently means putting another's interests ahead of one's own. Valuing another this much requires getting to know him or her and developing feelings of attachment and concern for that person. Ethical attitudes toward others may be considered an extension of our self-love (our survival instinct). The graph of a person's ethical development resembles a set of concentric circles, with the most immediate concerns closest to the center: oneself, followed by one's family and other close supporters, followed next by more distant relatives, more distant friends, acquaintances, strangers who bear strong resemblance to us or who are linked to us by common cultural or religious ties, then other strangers, and, finally, perceived enemies. When I recognize another as similar to or related to me, I feel associated with him or her and therefore I will more probably respond to that person with respect and care. Social interaction is our chance to learn over and over again that all people share some traits and seek the same goals. As we discover more about the place of our species in the universe, we may include in our concentric circles the rest of the animal kingdom and perhaps the entire universe. We meet people, learn about them, and act on our ethical systems through social interaction. By widening our social contacts we formulate an expansive, inclusive system of ethical beliefs.

Sexual Roles

Sexual roles have traditionally affected ethics by dividing the human family according to kind of work and, to use the kindest term possible, perceived differences in temperament. Although much has been done to erase the traditional boundaries, the residue of centuries of very narrow thinking still haunts both our images of our own sex and our images of the opposite sex. How we think we are supposed to act and how we think the other is supposed to act still limits our possibilities and, at times, even imprisons us in jobs or relationships that are detrimental to our self-esteem and continuing maturation. How each of the sexes approaches morality has generally been treated as necessarily different: because each experiences relationships from a different perspective, it has simply been assumed that each would also have a different role to play in the formation and exercise of the ethical virtues. The feminine role has historically included nurturing, helping, caring for others, tending to relationships, fostering values, and generally expressing the more emotional side of the human person. The masculine role has traditionally included the more assertive, intellectual, competitive, task-oriented, rational side of the species. The lines are no longer so brightly drawn, but we are far from obliterating the prejudice and narrow-mindedness that these stereotypical roles represent. Even the sexual revolution of the 1960s did not end the double standard, nor did it eliminate society's presumption that, at least in the domestic sphere, it falls to women to remain ethically strong while being more emotionally committed. Because society construes ethical and altruistic acts as more emotionally motivated, it expects women naturally to act more ethically and

altruistically. Society expects men to exhibit those ethical qualities that apply to their sphere—fairness in business dealings,
courage in adversity or danger, a strong work ethic, and so on.
It does not necessarily expect men to exhibit great emotional
care for others or empathy or nurturing—qualities it attributes
to women. In familial relationships, men have been perceived
to be the protectors, the breadwinners, the ones to face the
world and wrest from it the material goods necessary for the
family's survival.

In other words, besides dealing with the great confusion
that society's messages about sexual roles cause in our pursuit
of self-esteem, love, and meaning, we must also contend with
the havoc wreaked on our ethical systems by our preconceived
notions of what our sex dictates about our ethical selves.
Society's expectations and assumptions about sexual differences will necessarily infect one's self-image and, therefore,
one's ethical beliefs, but, like other influences we have considered, these expectations need not be final and controlling.
The impact of others' expectations and condemnation can
always be evaluated for its useful and appropriate elements, if
there are any, or can be minimized, if the notions are simply
destructive and debilitating.

Self-determination

Unbeknownst to most of us, we are all equipped with particular
philosophical temperaments or predispositions that guide us as
we attend to and interpret the world around us. Because most
of us lack extensive formal training in philosophical methods,
we mistakenly assume that we are not philosophical in our intellectual dealings. The most basic philosophical orientations are,
first and foremost, matters of temperament: not sophisticated
theories acquired through education and training, but rather
an apparently natural and basic intellectual apparatus that we
use to sort out the data and draw the conclusions that compose
our axioms. We use these axioms to form our ethical theories.
To speak of self-determination here is deceptive, because our
selves are not really under our own control. Our philosophical
temperaments are apparently built into our psychological

make-ups, and, although we can consciously identify and study them, we do not consciously choose these orientations. We can labor to minimize their weaknesses, but our conscious control is still limited and I doubt that one can reverse, in adulthood, one's ethical position should one even wish to try. Our selves that are being called upon to take over the reins of our ethical development are not, it turns out, completely within our control either. As we become more autonomous, we become aware of social and psychological data that originate outside ourselves, but which we experience as part of our very selves. This internalized data informs some of our most pervasive attitudes toward ourselves and other people.

These philosophical temperaments can be described in numerous ways, but I find the vocabulary and conceptual structure of the categories William James developed to be among the most clearly presented and intuitively straightforward, so I will use his terminology and distinctions in examining these most basic classes of orientation. Again, it should be emphasized that these temperaments are generalizations of the orientations that attract a person to one philosophy or ethical system rather than another. Like the axioms that lie at the root of our ethical systems, these orientations direct our thinking before we respond to a proposed theory or formally structured philosophical interpretation of experience. These most deepseated orientations dictate which of a number of equally sound theories "settles the question best for me." When logic dictates that a number of answers are equally plausible and explain the data satisfactorily, our personal philosophical orientations go to work and we choose on a deeper level, that is, by intuition.

The categories we will apply here are very broad, dividing the world of thinkers into two camps. This grossly simplified division is not intended to reveal the detailed characteristics of either camp, but you should be able to recognize the group into which you generally fall, and you will also, no doubt, recognize in the opposing group features that you have detected, but perhaps never specifically identified, in friends and colleagues.

The distinction between the two camps, tender-minded and tough-minded, is like what we call in common parlance the "forest versus the tree":[12]

The Tender-minded	The Tough-minded
Rationalistic (relying on principles)	Empiricist (relying on facts)
Intellectualistic	Sensationalistic
Idealistic	Materialistic
Optimistic	Pessimistic
Religious	Irreligious
Self-directed	Fatalistic
Monistic	Pluralistic
Dogmatical	Skeptical

Obviously you may find that you fall into one camp more than the other and yet nonetheless detect within your personality strong tendencies from the opposite list. This is not uncommon, but, as you consider how the composite is bound together, you may discover why some areas of tension or uneasy fit have been functioning within your makeshift system.

Neither camp is better or philosophically superior to the other: these are simply the two major divisions of temperaments, and each offers benefits and drawbacks. People with the tender-minded temperament see the forest rather than the trees. They always focus on the big picture, often losing significant detail in the process, and are much more likely to emphasize how all the seeming differences can be resolved into some unity. They are, therefore, drawn more to principles and intellectualized experience rather than the separate physical events of the concrete, material world. The tender-minded naturally perceive life as a monistic experience in which all individual experiences are part of the one, and unity is the most basic and genuine principle governing the universe. They are generally more religious because they seek a universal scheme of things that will resolve the messiness and separateness they encounter in their lives. For these people, to make sense of the world requires an answer that ties everything together in one neat package. The tender-minded are likewise inclined to be dogmatic because they respond more to theories and intellectualized versions of reality, which tend to be settled and solidified and, therefore, harder to dislodge and update, than they respond to the more rapidly changing realities encountered from day to day. As they gain

experience, tender-minded people cling to their former interpretation until the fit becomes too lopsided and they are so
stressed that they must undertake the unsettling job of rework-
ing the theory to accommodate the stubborn data. This is the
ideal case, of course: intellectually dishonest or simply uninter-
ested tender-minded thinkers will simply cling to the theory
regardless of the data. They will become dogmatists who have
lost touch with reality but are still attempting to make the data
fit the old ideas. Consider the extraordinary efforts made to
preserve the geocentric theory of the universe and the intellectual gymnastics performed to reinterpret the data to make
it obey the theory. The last general trait of the tender-minded,
optimism, can be traced to their trust in their big picture that
smoothes out the wrinkles and resolves contradictions and
conflicts in their experience. Their vision is always directed to
their big picture and seldom directed to the many little steps
and detours along the way.

Describing the tough-minded thinker is now a fairly simple
process: simply negating the tendencies described above gives
a pretty clear picture of this temperament. Tough-minded
thinkers are much more preoccupied with the separate facts
and the events that keep them rooted in their everyday experience and are less concerned with hunting for some
overarching explanation of how the pieces of the puzzle fit
together. The tough-minded are generally more detail-
oriented. They notice and appreciate the differences between
experiences and the multifaceted character of life.
Appreciation of the changeable and volatile aspects of the
world makes the tough-minded more skeptical and on guard
against settling for a theory that might neglect some significant distinctions or omit some of the rich detail that colors
experience and calls a theory to our attention in the first
place. These people are less likely to be religious, because
their experience remains grounded in the here and now and
does not seem to lend itself to some simple interpretation
such as a divine plan. Such a view may ignore what religious
thinkers see as the unpleasant or irreconcilable (and therefore evil) aspects of the universe, namely, contradictions and
imperfections. The tough-minded prefer to focus on concrete
experiences as the most immediate and reliable modes of

experience and shy away from excessive intellectualizing and theorizing. The tough-minded trust their experiences far more than the theories proposed to explain them.

After reading the description of the two camps, most people feel that the best temperament would capture the best of both worlds. We are all drawn at times to the strong features of the temperament opposite our own and, as James points out, our unsuccessful attempts at having it all create a hodgepodge system that works only so long as we are lucky enough to escape a collision of views on a single matter.

> Facts are good, of course—give us lots of facts. Principles are good—give us plenty of principles. The world is indubitably one if you look at in one way, but as [*sic*] indubitably many, if you look at it in another. It is both one and many—let us adopt a sort of pluralistic monism. Everything of course is necessarily determined, and yet of course our wills are free: a sort of free-will determinism is the true philosophy. The evil of the parts is undeniable, but the whole can't be evil: so practical pessimism can be combined with metaphysical optimism. And so forth— your ordinary philosophic layman never being a radical, never straightening out his system, but living vaguely in one plausible compartment of it or another to suit the temptations of successive hours.[13]

We cannot have it all, unfortunately, despite our best efforts, and so we settle into one temperament or the other as our stance toward the world, and then we work at resolving the problems that arise as we discover the gaps that either temperament creates. But this all occurs, for the most part, unconsciously, and very few people ever realize that they even have a particular philosophical temperament. On the contrary, they really do not experience their temperament at all, and they presume that the categories and biases it applies are neutral and, therefore, nonselective. They want to believe that any discrimination among data occurs later in our experiences, at the conscious level. Most of us head out into the world equipped with some individualized version of one of these two temperaments and then live as though the filters created by the temperament were standard equipment for all humans. We assume that everyone experiences the world and interprets experiences the way we do. However, what we describe as our experiences has already been subjected to sifting, filtering, choosing, rejecting, and so on long before it ever becomes part of our conscious experience.

Another way to classify temperament examines our duty in forming opinions and acquiring knowledge. We all need to know enough to function comfortably in the world. How far we develop intellectually beyond the minimally practical is then a matter of personal choice, ability, and ambition. But we all recognize that one must be on guard against the practical effects of error in our systems of belief: error frustrates our efforts, can contaminate true beliefs, and can leave us confused and unable to act effectively. However, in the matter of directing the process of forming opinions, two more discernible camps of philosophers emerge: those driven by a need to know the truth and those driven by a need to avoid error.[14] At first it appears that these two tendencies are two sides of the same coin and that to accomplish one is to accomplish the other. But, in fact, the preoccupation of each temperament is drastically at odds with that of the other and reveals an opposite orientation toward what constitutes responsible thinking and acting in the world.

People driven to know the truth are generally open to experience from all quarters, mindful always that truth may lie in unexpected places, and therefore, like Diogenes who endlessly wandered in search of the honest person, such people are constantly moving on, welcoming and intentionally seeking new, broader experiences and new theories, always searching for the most complete experience and all-encompassing worldview. Mistakes for such people are an inevitable and minor part of the process: to capture the most truth, one also must tolerate a certain amount, even a large amount, of error. But what really counts is how many truths are discovered, not how many errors get mixed in along the way.

But people who are driven by the duty to avoid error find themselves much more wary and more cautious. These people seek as many truths as they can with the minimum number of errors. These people cannot be as carefree and expansive about offbeat or foreign experiences, methods, and intellectual systems. They feel they are graded on wrong answers as heavily as on right ones, so they must, above all, be cautious in what they believe. In the development of their opinions, they test and retest a view many times before they include it in their small but thoroughly verified system of beliefs. Being duped becomes the ultimate nightmare, and therefore these people are apprehensive and on guard rather than open and trustful of others and their views.

The differences between these two orientations create differences in attitude that affect areas of life that seem to have little connection with how people form opinions and acquire knowledge. These attitudes subtly program people's responsiveness to and openness toward those around them.

Therefore, even if we, as adults, elect to take charge of our own lives and ethical views, we still discover that what we have experienced as very personal and private feelings and intuitions about the world are actually the result of some very subtle programming from within and from without. But this does not destroy for any of us the opportunity to develop greater autonomy.

None of us has the luxury of embarking on self-determination with a blank slate and a perfectly intact intellectual and emotional apparatus. We are all slowly making our way, trying to clear a path and determine a new direction with only minimally functional tools. But the picture is not as bleak as it may appear. A much greater degree of self-determination can be gained by anyone willing to persevere despite the social pressures to give in and blindly follow traditional wisdom. The sorting process is not without support and guidance. Each of us depends on a blend of the methods of correspondence and coherence in reshaping our ethical systems. Correspondence is the check we perform on our axioms: What, exactly, are my deepest beliefs about myself, my world? Are my impressions accurate? For example, consider my belief that a particular expressway leads to a particular town. To test for correspondence I need only take the journey. Some beliefs, however, even in the empirical realm, cannot be tested so easily, for example, the belief that light is a particle rather than a wave.

Because I lack the expertise to directly test this belief for correspondence with reality, I turn to coherence tests. Does the belief that light is a particle fit better with my ideas about particles than it does with my ideas about waves?

When testing new ideas we perform both tests if possible. If the idea fails either test, we are apt to reject the idea as false. If coherence is not easily ascertained, then one should perform the following test: envision some behaviors that would result from adopting these axioms. Draw out as many instances of consequences as possible. Now, compare the results. If the axioms yield compatible results, then the system most probably exhibits coherence, but if conflicts and contradictions in expected behavior arise, then the axioms are in conflict and attempts to juggle them will only frustrate the person who operates within this ethical system. Then one must identify the opposing axioms and weigh their importance to the system as a whole. What is the ultimate arbiter as one attempts to choose between two cherished but contradictory beliefs? For most of us, the axiom that will be retained will be the one that fits most smoothly with and supports our other most cherished beliefs. Relinquishing any comfortable, secure belief is not easy, but any idea can grow comfortable if held long enough whether it makes any real sense or not. The comfortable becomes for us indistinguishable from the true simply because as long as an idea is not tested, mere familiarity with it can endear it to us, regardless of its actual applicability or relevance to our experiences.

Coherence and correspondence work together to ensure that our beliefs are grounded in our realities and that our belief system is a consistent and reliable map of our world and experience. Self-determination requires, above all else, that one continually entertain the possibility that one's beliefs may not be true and may need to be replaced with ideas that may initially strike one as strange. But the good news is that as one discards the erroneous or outdated axioms and beliefs and replaces them with consciously adopted ones, one acts with ease and assurance because now the ideas actually fit one's experience and reflect one's relationship with reality.

The choice is not strictly between self-determination and other-determination. We are repeatedly bombarded with others' influences, even after we assert ourselves and direct our own systems of belief. The realistic goal is to be primarily self-determined and self-directed and more selective in adopting the beliefs held out by others. We cannot escape others' influence, even if we want to; in fact, they often provide us with invaluable positive feedback and prod us into thinking about some of our outdated views in new and interesting ways. Our independently chosen ethical systems might very strongly resemble the system that we had merely absorbed before, simply because some ideas are still valid and valuable. This process is not primarily destructive, but rather an exercise in critical analysis and scrupulous honing: what proves true should be kept, regardless of its source, but, likewise, what proves false and destructive must be parted with, regardless of its familiarity and emotional appeal. One cannot carry around useless and false notions because, when one must act, they will prove frustrating and will thwart our efforts to achieve a good and productive ethical life.

Self-determination is an ongoing process, completed only when individuals have had their last experience and their lives are over. One does not attain a complete, forever-closed system of ethical beliefs any more than one creates a final version of one's personality or perspective. One's system, like one's personality, is sensitive to new experiences, new relationships, and new events. Growth is essential, not threatening, to the system, and exercising one's beliefs provides the surest means of exposing error, undue influence from unreliable sources, and passive acceptance of useless baggage.

Selecting a Standard: What Is the Good Life?

Difficulties in Identifying the Good

All approaches to ethical issues seem to share one characteristic: preoccupation with the good life. Philosophers have approached that question from some very different perspectives and have attributed to humans some markedly different qualities, talents, needs, and desires. But pursuing the ethically good connotes genuine living, realizing one's best potential; in short, living not only a good life, but the best life possible.

Identifying what we consider best and most desirable for ourselves would seem at first to be a foolishly simple exercise. After all, we all seem to intuitively grasp what philosophers have traditionally termed the problem of evil, and we all question, at one time or another, why things must go wrong. No one seems to experience any problem of good, and yet I have discovered, through teaching philosophy of religion over the years and in examining students' notions of what they thought heaven—the model of perfect existence—would be like, that many people have a naive, undeveloped and simplistic notion of the good life.

In an episode of the very popular television series, "The Twilight Zone," written by Rod Serling, a gangster found himself trapped at the dead end of an alley, chased by a rival gang. As they drew their guns and opened fire on him he closed his eyes and dropped to the ground. A few seconds later he opened his eyes in amazement. The thugs were gone and a lone man, a stranger, faced him. The bewildered gangster stood up and commented that it was incredible that all the thugs had missed when they fired at him. The stranger replied that the thugs did not miss and that he would accompany the deceased gangster to his new abode. For a moment the gangster feared that he would now have to pay for a life misspent, but before he could indulge in much self-pity or remorse, he found himself and his guide in the doorway of an elegant casino—gambling had been his favorite pastime—and the stranger told him that he could, for all eternity, place his bets and never lose. In addition, the quite beautiful women the gangster saw inside would find him irresistible and would never say no to any request he might make. The gangster, of course, marveled at his luck at apparently being mistaken for someone else and being assigned that person's reward. But, as time passed, he became discontented as he realized that his enjoyment of gambling had hinged on the genuine possibility of loss or failure. He loved these activities because he sought in them a chance to beat the odds. It was not just winning more money or controlling more women; he needed to know that he had won the money and conquered the women. Here there were no odds to beat: he could never lose, and therefore he also could never win. He became so frustrated that he confronted the stranger and exclaimed in exasperation, "What kind of a heaven *is* this?" The stranger replied, "Why, sir, whatever made you think this was *heaven?*"

We have all experienced the disappointment of getting exactly what we thought we desired most, only to find that it did not bring us the intense satisfaction that we had so anxiously longed for. Most of us, for example, would never write disappointment or anxiety onto our blueprint for a happy life, even though much of our learning and self-exploration occurs when we are frustrated or challenged. Like the child who pictures heaven as endless dessert, continuously running cartoons and no bedtime, we distort our projections of the good life with misguided and infantile notions of human nature, as well as satisfaction and happiness.

Aldous Huxley's *Brave New World* depicted an ideal society in which all human frustration and anxiety had been eliminated, taking with them the need for genuine human endeavor and growth. The civilization worked for virtually all its inhabitants, who were programmed to appreciate their surroundings and position in life; but, despite the government's best efforts, occasional misfits were born who seemed incapable of assimilation. These freethinkers posed such a threat that they had to be either exiled or annihilated. Toward the end of the book, one such misfit, called the Savage, who was visiting from what was considered a much more primitive society, was brought before the head of the state, the Controller, to learn what his fate would be. The Controller argued in favor of the virtues of uninterrupted social stability and continuous happiness, which, as they both agreed, required the removal of any genuine challenges and difficulties. The Savage argued for the life that would allow people to experience their highest nature and true, albeit sporadic, happiness. The Savage had observed continuous happiness and had been disillusioned by the mediocrity of the people's lives. Instead of enjoying what we in our culture would call the fine arts, the reflection of humankind's soul—namely, arts, music, and literature—the people were constantly bombarded with the most innocuous and shallow distractions and were never exposed to any ideas or artistic expressions that would stimulate thought or deep emotion. The Savage even asked the Controller why the people could not be allowed to experience the truly beautiful and deeply moving aspects of life—for example, great literature like *Othello*. The Controller replied that the people of his society, in their completely happy and contented state, would simply not be able to understand it. And when the Savage pressed him to explain why this would be so, he replied:

> Because our world is not the same as Othello's world. You can't make flivvers without steel—and you can't make tragedies without social instability. The world's stable now. People are happy; they get what they want, and they never want what they can't get. They're well off; they're safe; they're never ill; they're not afraid of death; they're blissfully ignorant of passion and old age; they're plagued with no mothers or fathers; they've got no wives, or children, or loves to feel strongly about; they're so conditioned that they

practically can't help behaving as they ought to behave. And if anything should go wrong, there's *soma* [a drug]. Which you go and chuck out of the window in the name of liberty, Mr. Savage. *Liberty!* . . . Expecting [lower-class citizens] to know what liberty is! And now expecting them to understand *Othello!* My good boy![1]

At that point, the Savage, noticeably unimpressed with the Controller's choice of priorities, remarked that from his standpoint it all still seemed quite horrible and not at all what one would truly want, to which the Controller replied:

Actual happiness always looks pretty squalid in comparison with the over-compensations for misery. And, of course, stability isn't nearly so spectacular as instability. And being contented has none of the glamour of a good fight against misfortune, none of the picturesqueness of a struggle with temptation, or a fatal overthrow by passion or doubt. Happiness is never grand.[2]

The Savage argued that our species desires not only comfort and good feelings, which we often mistake for genuine happiness, but also the opportunity to earn real happiness. It can be said of our species that we value and cherish whatever we enjoy in this life in proportion to what we endured to obtain it. Anything that comes too easily will be enjoyed, perhaps, but not esteemed and truly valued. He then attempted to explain this concept to the Controller through references to his own culture.

"There's a story one of the old Indians used to tell us, about the Girl of Matasaki. The young men who wanted to marry her had to do a morning's hoeing in her garden. It seemed easy; but there were flies and mosquitoes, magic ones. Most of the young men simply couldn't stand the biting and stinging. But the one that could—he got the girl."

"Charming! But in civilized countries," said the Controller, "you can have girls without hoeing for them; and there aren't any flies or mosquitoes to sting you. We got rid of them all centuries ago."

The Savage nodded, frowning:

"You got rid of them. Yes, that's just like you. Getting rid of everything unpleasant instead of learning to put up with it. 'Whether 'tis nobler in the mind to suffer the slings and arrows of outrageous fortune, or to take arms against a sea of troubles and by opposing end them . . .' But you don't do either. Neither suffer nor oppose. You just abolish the slings and arrows. It's too easy. . . . What you need . . . is something *with* tears for a change. Nothing costs enough here."[3]

In the end, one of the genetic engineers on the Controller's staff, pondering the implications of the Savage's value system, stated: "In fact, you're claiming the right to be unhappy." And the Savage replied, "All right, then . . . I'm claiming the right to be unhappy."[4] Like the gangster and the Savage, we all experience times when we wish we faced less work, fewer problems, more modest challenges, but a life entirely without such hurdles is probably not what we dream it would be, nor would we be as happy and contented in the long run as we imagine. We are a species coded for trial and error, and yet we long for a life without work, error, disappointment, sickness, or imperfection. We behave as the moth that hovers, fascinated, over the flame and draws closer and closer to destruction. What we long for is destructive to our most basic tendencies, urges, and powers: we want the glory of victory without the possibility of defeat, and that is a logical contradiction.

John Dewey, in his work *Quest for Certainty*, traced the evolution of human consciousness as a response to problems and hostile changes in our environment. In other words, as a species we would never have become conscious beings if we had not been forced to constantly face scarcity and other threats of destruction. Our desire for certainty, rather than some mysterious metaphysical urge or lofty philosophical goal, has proven a quite natural trait with an overwhelming power for our survival. Change should cause us anxiety and get our attention, because the being that fails to notice an approaching enemy or threat will not live long. We want uncertainty banished because that means mastery over those threatening elements of our environment that we cannot control. Knowledge truly is power when it successfully predicts an enemy's move and shows us how to counter it or escape it. Human abstract thought—our capacity to anticipate and generalize—coupled with our drive to know and to attain certainty has provided us the best chances of success as a species. But, as a species, we also need to have challenges, at least some mild threats to our survival, and goals to actively pursue if we are to draw on our human powers, skills, and faculties. The good life must be a balanced life, providing both stimuli for growth and change and intermittent periods of stability, satisfaction, and contentment.

Distinguishing between the Good and the Perfect

Perfection, which we visualize as ultimate goodness, total satisfaction, and complete safety, is actually anathema to our deepest drives. We equate lack of perfection with failure, but, for our finite species and for every other species that shares our earthly existence, the good and the imperfect are intertwined. Evolution has depended on imperfection—and would have been impossible without it.

> This principle does not apply to humans only. It permeates creation. It is the very stuff of which evolution is made. Take the amphibians. The first one that crawled out of the water onto the land may not have done so because its feet were so strong, but because its gills were so weak. The imperfection of its gills made that first amphibian into an animal of a higher order. But one can imagine its parents' distress at having a child that was so conspicuously unable to live a normal aquatic life, a child with which there was obviously something wrong, and one can imagine how it was jeered at by its peers. Nor did that first amphibian have any idea that its 'wrongness' had led it into a 'betterness.'[5]

If living well means pursuing the life that will draw out our greatest abilities, then the good life will necessarily include work, real losses, disappointments, mistakes, and plenty of imperfection. We mistake our roots and misread our history when we posit as the good life—the life we were meant to live—the life of constant satisfaction and absolute perfection.

We have evolved scientists . . . and so we know a lot about DNA, but if our kind of mind had been confronted with the problem of designing a similar replicating molecule . . . we'd have never succeeded. We would have made one fatal mistake: our molecule would have been perfect. . . . The capacity to blunder slightly is the real marvel of DNA. Without this special attribute we would still be anaerobic bacteria and there would be no music.[6]

As a species, we still long to return to the Garden of Eden, where we believe we were actually intended to live and for which we believe we were originally designed. We cling to the notion that strife, competition, and disequilibrium are truly out of place in our lives and destructive to our essence, while the plateaus of calm, serenity, and contentment reflect our truer natures and genuine human existence. We posit the perfect as the only worthwhile and acceptable goal and then are surprised and disappointed that life fails to meet our expectations. We presume that life cannot be good unless it can be perfect. However, the two terms are not synonymous. It is a noble enough endeavor for us to strive for the good life without demanding a perfect one, which will never come. The varieties of truly good lives are still endless. The following is a sample of the good as posited throughout the history of philosophy. Individuals must posit their own good and then fashion an ethical system around it. The value of these ready-made philosophies is that you can adopt and adapt any features that fit well within your own framework.

Traditional Interpretations of the Good

Although every discipline has a bearing on the quality of humankind's existence, philosophy has traditionally addressed the question "What constitutes the good life?" Common themes have recurred throughout the history of philosophy, but, as humankind has developed—not necessarily progressed—how individuals in different eras and in different cultures have interpreted that crucial term *good* has been markedly different. Each has polished a facet of the stone. Every view offers some value;

even those we find unsuitable now may nonetheless prove relevant later. For those who shy away from the works of the ancients, for example, on the grounds that they are, after all, ancient, I can only say that we humans have always recognized, for example, our own mortality, our need for love and self-esteem, and the continuing tensions between reason and the emotions and that we can learn from the efforts of others, even those far removed from us in history.

In their attempts to identify the highest good of humankind—what makes a life worthwhile—philosophers have tried to shorten the lists of goods to reach that one ultimate, best Good. For Plato, that was the rationally regulated life, one in which reason controlled a person's other faculties. For Aristotle, Happiness proved the supreme value that was sought for its own sake. Epicurus designated Pleasure as humankind's goal, viewing all actions as motivated by either attraction to pleasure or aversion to pain. Conspicuously absent from the ethical theories is a simple answer to the question "What constitutes the good life?"

Understanding a concept as elusive as the meaning and purpose of life requires that we recognize the principles we generally accept to guide our search. That we are mortal creatures colors our analysis of the quality of any particular lifework or life-style. Because we can be self-conscious and anticipate our own deaths, we feel driven to both live life to the fullest and get our houses in order. Our species plans for the future while it lives in the present. Any standards of the good life we accept must apply to both our present and our future.

So, first of all, to speak of the good life is to refer to the whole life—life considered in its entirety—not only isolated moments here and there. We may have to compromise: we may sacrifice pleasures that offer intense enjoyment in the present if they frustrate our cherished, long-term goals. We perceive the good life as the one guaranteeing pleasure and security throughout our lives, and most of us will not seriously jeopardize our futures for a few hours, days, or weeks of even extremely intense pleasure.

A requirement stressed by Aristotle is that our ultimate value or goal be recognizable by its intrinsic worth to us. For a value to define the good life, it must be valuable for its own sake, not because it will enable us to reach another goal. In that case, the first value is not the ultimate quality or state sought but is merely a means to reach the ultimate goal. What makes life worthwhile, what our ultimate good is, must be recognizable throughout one's life (although not necessarily at every moment) and must be recognizable as a final, intrinsically valuable goal.

Simple answers like good health or money do not suffice for most people because, although each value can contribute to a good life, it does not seem to be the final goal. Physical comfort for most would be desirable but not sufficient to make a lifetime worthwhile or good. Most of us have endured great pain during our lifetimes and yet would agree that, for the right goal, enduring great pain might be acceptable. But if absence of pain is the ultimate good, then nothing can justify voluntarily enduring great physical pain or discomfort. The act would either be irrational or totally stupid, because a rational person would not sacrifice a greater good for a lesser one. Even money, often cited by people of all economic backgrounds as the supreme good, generally fails to meet our criteria. Money is desired because it brings its owner something else of value: it is seldom coveted for itself. If money can buy freedom or security or power, then those are the values and money represents merely the means to obtain them.

Thus our search will meet the requirements we humans have for finality and thoroughness, but that is only the beginning. Certain additional restraints and demands reflect tastes and preferences that originate both within and without the individual, both consciously and unconsciously, and also reflect beliefs about the way the world works and the way humans can, or cannot, fit into it.

All concepts of the good life have reflected and incorporated their creators' optimism and confidence in humankind. Some have seen our species' role as chiefly that of discoverer of values already in existence. The ancient Greeks saw humankind's control over the physical world and the realm of ideas and values as minimal: we can recognize the good, but cannot participate in its creation. In contrast, the existentialists, writing in the late nineteenth and early twentieth centuries, attributed to humans much more extensive power to impose their own values onto nature and to contribute to the human endeavor of making sense of the world. Just as one can observe in the history of art the impact that scientific advancement has had on humans' powers of perception and perspective through artists' use of color and light, the study of different philosophers shows us how our sense of our place in and power over nature influences our understanding of what is truly best and most desirable.

The Albert Brooks film *Defending Your Life* echoed this theme and depicted an afterlife in which everyone could eat as much as he or she wanted and yet never gain weight (as being overweight is a preoccupation in the United States in the 1990s it naturally has worked its way into our notion of the perfect afterlife) while experiencing an enhanced sense of taste and, therefore, greater enjoyment of food. The more substantial issue was what behavior earns for humans a place in this perfect afterlife. The film portrayed an interesting shift in our thinking about ourselves and in the form that modern-day "sin" takes. The panel of evaluators who assessed the value of each decedent's life conducted the hearing much as we conduct a criminal trial, although they staunchly maintained that the defendants should not view the process as a legal procedure. However, each decedent was supplied with counsel who argued in favor of eternal reward, while the afterlife society provided a prosecutor who argued that the person had not yet earned the reward. The evidence included moments in the person's life chosen to reveal the person's significant qualities and to prove the candidate worthy. Those qualities were not the golden rule or Ten Commandments variety, but instead concerned the person's struggle with his or her own fears, indecisiveness, and stupidity. Humans were to be judged not on how well they comported themselves according to some externally imposed rules and regulations, but rather on how well they conquered themselves and their insecurities and inadequacies. The impact of our current preoccupation with self-help and self-actualization is unmistakable in this film. As we unite these newer standards with our more traditional views of our goals and values, the resulting definition of the good life will no doubt represent our collective and individual experiences up to this moment.

In other words, a person's notion of the good life will necessarily incorporate more than strictly philosophical concepts. A culture's scientific, religious, artistic, and sociological values shape the individual who posits the goal. And, therefore, our culture's biases influence our unconscious, unexamined beliefs and attitudes about our potential to grow and do good and to select appropriate and feasible goals. Often the cultural influence is so insidious that we are unaware of it. Several years ago, I was examining an alternative text for my introductory philosophy course. When I came to the unit addressing philosophical issues of belief in God I was intellectually jarred by the title: "Are There Gods?" My cultural bias toward monotheism would have led me to pose the question in the singular, thereby unintentionally guiding the reader, by my linguistic device, to follow the same path that I trod.

Every culture has fashioned its version of the good life by selecting what it perceived to be the best human features and then envisioning the environment in which those features could flourish and develop to the individual's best advantage. Each culture has responded to its people's most pressing problems, most persistent needs and shortcomings, and most cherished values and dreams. The examples below attempt to identify the good life—our ideal existence—as characterized in the Western tradition. The list is not exhaustive but includes most of the major schools of thought. For each I have merely explained the standard beliefs in modern terms rather than presented the views through the thoughts of the pertinent philosophers. In some cases, the theories of several thinkers who held similar views but enhanced different features are treated as a single composite theory; the superstructure is attributable to no single individual because it combines the work of many philosophers.

The Good as Happiness

Alexis de Tocqueville, when making his extensive study of the rapidly growing culture in the United States in the nineteenth century, is said to have remarked on what he perceived as the most peculiar fact—that we have built into our notions of fundamental rights those of "life, liberty and the pursuit of happiness." What he found particularly odd was the fact that happiness, as he understood it, was more an indirect goal than a goal that could be directly pursued. Many philosophers have shared his observation, noting that the term *happiness* actually covers a multitude of experiences and indicates merely the overall quality of the composite. However, despite its somewhat intangible, amorphous quality, most of us would pin the term *happiness* to the quality of life that we hold out as the best good.

However, simply using the same term for our ultimate good is not enough. Leonard Bernstein's *Candide* contains a hilariously funny, but also tragically familiar, scene in which the two lovers, Candide and Cunegonde, stand professing their love to one another, staring out into the future in opposite directions. They both sing of the qualities of the good life—he, of a rustic, simple existence on a farm where they would raise pigs; she, of the fine life in exotic cities, moving from grand party to grand party—each woefully oblivious to what the other is saying. Near the close of the duet, they turn back, once again gazing into each other's eyes, and sing about how wonderful it is that they agree completely. The audience is thus prepared for the frustration and inevitable disappointment that lie ahead for the doomed couple. If we take happiness to be the ultimate good, and we understand that the term can easily represent radically different settings and modes of realization for different individuals, then we should not be surprised to find a myriad of different ethical systems throughout even a single culture. How one ought to live to maximize the good necessarily will differ as the individual's notion of true happiness differs. No system is perfect, but a review of our human needs and expectations with respect to our experience of ethics quickly reveals the strong points and shortcomings of building an ethical system based on happiness as the guiding principle.

Appealing to a principle like happiness as an ultimate guide avoids wrestling with a more esoteric, other-worldly standard that may defy reason or at least confuse and complicate the process. The particulars of happiness may differ from one person to another, but, at least within an individual's system, the mystery and guesswork can be cleared up by refining the individual's expression of his or her deepest, most compelling desires. Individuals consider their goals to lie in the strictly human sphere, and, although no doubt a common thread runs through the system over a lifetime, because the ultimate goal is expected to change the system will not be rigid. Flexibility, concreteness, and individuality are this system's strongest points, and they satisfy some of our emotional demands but not some other psychological and emotional demands.

As mentioned earlier, we experience ethical dictates not only as our preferences or dislikes, but also as objective standards, applicable to others as well. Positing my version of happiness makes my ethical system subjective, individualistic, and flexible, but it does not provide an objective, permanent anchor to keep the ethical "I ought" from collapsing into a mere "I enjoy" or "I like." That I value relationships and take great pains to understand, empathize with, and care for others and obey a strong ethical command to treat others fairly reflects only on my version of happiness. People whose concepts of happiness do not stress relationships might act differently toward me. Therefore, although each of us might be responding to the other in a rational, ethically appropriate, and consistent manner, we both could be disappointed, frustrated, and unhappy. Without some agreement, our systems of belief represent what we want but not necessarily what we mean by what one ought to want or ought to do. If happiness is the ultimate standard, then we cannot even comment on the relative merit of various individuals' definitions to resolve the discord. After individuals claim that their actions are in accord with their ultimate standard of happiness, no further argument can be offered.

Some philosophers have attempted to avoid this inevitable clash of interests by positing happiness as the ultimate principle only when considered to apply to the whole group, not the individual. They reformulate the principle as the greatest happiness for the greatest number, or some similar phrase, so that there is some means of measuring the ethical appropriateness of an individual's acts by evaluating their impact on the collective happiness. This move seems to give the system objectivity and stability, but the capriciousness of the individual is simply replaced by the capriciousness of the majority. Happiness must be carefully defined, should one decide to adopt it as one's standard, and simplistic notions of "what feels good" or "what I like to do" must be replaced with more objective, permanent values. Shortsighted systems provide plenty of room for subjectivity but no means of incorporating the objective. Both sets of demands are psychologically compelling to us because we need flexibility and stability, but the most flexible and subjective systems are the least stable and objective.

This does not mean that one must abandon one's system for an all-inclusive one; there is no such system—at least not yet. None of the standards I analyze here have ever answered all our needs and satisfied all our demands. The best one can do is to decide, at the outset, which demands are most critical to oneself, and then construct a system that will address them. Faults and imperfections are inevitable because the system is a finite system created by a finite being, but that should encourage one to be open-minded and keep adjusting the system.

Some major philosophers have believed that happiness is the only possible base for an ethical system. One of the earliest philosophers to develop this notion of the good was Aristotle. Aristotle observed the choices of those around him and attempted to identify their motivations. He concluded that happiness is the ultimate goal of humanity, the only goal sought and valued for itself alone and not as a means to a more important goal. However, Aristotle believed that happiness could be attained only by developing and exercising human virtues. His emphasis on virtue as excellence paralleled Plato's notion but expanded it. (Plato's approach is considered in the next section.) Aristotle recognized the importance of rational virtues and knowledge but realized that most people live their lives without much true intellection, responding out of habit rather than thought. Aristotle therefore posited that the good life and, therefore, the life of happiness, was a matter of good habits exercised in accord with rational principles that would be grasped by the few but lived out by the many. In other words, individuals experience happiness in accord with their understanding and intellectual power. Aristotle did not consider happiness like the superficial, pleasant sensation experienced by the characters in Huxley's *Brave New World,* but rather he assessed the quality of a person's life in terms of ultimate happiness: a life consisting of its share of work, worries, and problems, but guided by good values and good friends and complete with self-esteem, education, love, and respect for one's fellows. Happiness would be an objective and objectively verifiable standard, less flexible but more stable and objective than the standards of other systems.

Furthermore, happiness, as the ultimate value, is final in that it is sought for its own sake and self-sufficient in that it is enough to create a complete life. Finality and self-sufficiency have often been selected as the natural basis of a humanly conceived ethical system, but it is not sufficiently objective, universal, or, for even the single subscriber, stable.

The Good as Rational Virtue

Plato devoted his philosophical career to answering the question "What is the good life?" as it applied both to the individual and to society. Through introspection and observation of those around him, Plato determined that, as a species, humans have three distinct faculties that work together at times but at other times are more like warring factions. In modern terms, we might refer to these faculties as the rational, the biological, and the emotional. Each drives us toward what it expects will be pleasurable or away from what it considers painful, but the wisdom of the respective faculties' choices differs widely. Reason outstrips both the others in dependability and farsightedness. Plato believed that our emotions and passions, while noble and necessary in an individual's life, prompt us to obtain short-lived pleasure but not lasting satisfaction. Only one's reason acknowledges the priority of lasting values and restrains our fleeting thoughts in moments of anxiety, exhilaration, and passion. Current literature in popular psychology presents a similar thesis: that emotionally balanced people who recognize the long-term consequences of their behaviors and desires can choose wisely and, therefore, suffer less in the long run. The key in these systems, however, is definitely a well-developed intellect. Reason is the key to the good life in Plato's system.

This approach assumes that humans are rather passive. The intellect does not create the values or the rules. Reason merely reveals what is best, and then it is up to the person to act accordingly. Plato had a deep trust that people would naturally feel drawn to what is the best action or behavior for them. He believed that learning to reason rather than adopting the best path was the real struggle for people. Many of us, particularly those of us who have chosen the teaching profession, make this major mistake: we presume that our students will naturally respond to the knowledge we present once they intellectually grasp its significance. However, as we all learn, knowing what is truly best for us does not guarantee that we will behave according to the standard. Anyone who tries to diet or give up an unhealthy habit learns this quickly. We frequently are willing to settle for a short-term pleasure at the expense of an obviously superior long-term benefit. But despite his optimism about the human rational faculty, Plato did recommend considering the lasting benefit when choosing among competing pleasures: when the faculties oppose each other, one should select the most permanent.

Although few today would cite rational virtue as the embodiment of their view of the good life, Plato's concept of the divided self and its conflicting drives does provide some useful insight into what blocks achievement of that desired state. Perhaps attaining rational virtue seems more like pursuing the means rather than the end, but for Plato rational virtue was the sole means of even embarking on a genuine life journey. In his view, for individuals to achieve the good life, they must first master the rational virtues. All other pursuits paled by comparison.

The Good as Freedom and the Creation of Value

The existentialists are the preeminent philosophers who posit freedom and the creation of value as the crux of the good life. To adopt their mind-set actually requires a significant shift in one's thinking about what is normally associated with the term *good*. Traditional philosophers who reject the entire existentialist movement as an insult to legitimate philosophy on the grounds that it is, after all, practically anti-intellectual and purely subjective in its stance on philosophical questions must nonetheless acknowledge that existentialist thinkers provide a thoroughgoing, intensely individualistic worldview that is emotionally quite compelling and liberating—however pessimistic and negative the conclusions may appear.

Jean-Paul Sartre, in his play *No Exit,* described hell and the pursuits that are likely to condemn one to such a fate. The broader implication of the play, however, is that a hellish state is already available as an ongoing misery in this life.[7] The characters of the story are confused by their demise and nervous as they wait for word of their fate. As they converse about their lives and reveal their particular loves, hates, and drives, it becomes obvious that each person desires, needs, or is attracted to a quality or ability that another person has and could offer to and thereby help fulfill that person. However, it is equally obvious that because of the second party's loves, hates, and drives, he or she will forever deny the first party's most fervent wish. The result, of course, is a true hell that capitalizes on each person's desperation, insecurities, and weaknesses. As the waiting is dragged out and no word is received about their fates, the main character realizes and reveals to the others that what they have construed to be a way station is their final destination. They are one another's hell.

This bleak picture is not without its positive side. Sartre attempted to liberate humankind from objective, externally imposed values and to reveal that the sine qua non of our existence has really always been our ability to dictate exactly what the values are: to create values and, in so doing, determine how we should spend our lives. It is not fate or a god or nature that dictates what should count to us as valuable: we decide that for ourselves. It is our creative ability that makes human beings the masters of our fates: events merely occur and are neither good nor bad until humans declare them to be so. A life is a series of moments filled with activities that possess no importance; humans have the power to create values.

Evaluating the good life is a very different analysis under the existentialist approach. Precisely what I did and which circumstances fell to me in life have only secondary importance. What I did with the raw material, how I valued it, and what I added to the indifferent events in my life by creating and imposing a value structure are of primary importance.

In his *Myth of Sisyphus*, Albert Camus pushes the analysis one step further by positing what he took to be the most base, most futile existence, and yet—by using the existentialist approach—he re-created and reinterpreted that life to give it value. Sisyphus had been condemned by the gods to ceaselessly roll a rock up to the top of a mountain. Then it would roll back down under its own weight, and Sisyphus would have to roll it up again. He would work forever without any tangible results: no achievement, no rest, no end, no purpose. Camus points out that the real punishment was not the futile labor, which he believed many of his fellows endured daily, but rather that Sisyphus was conscious of the futility. Sisyphus becomes a tragic figure because he knows that he cannot change his fate and will never complete the task the gods assigned to him. Yet Camus comments, "One must imagine Sisyphus happy,"[8] because he can willingly and freely embrace whatever fate sends his way. He always retains the power to say yes and to accept the circumstances of his life. Making a commitment to accept and live one's life creates value where there was none before, and the act need not depend on life being good or circumstances being favorable. All that is required is the freedom to think on one's own and the commitment to create and affix one's stamp of approval and value on the circumstances or on the life as a whole.

The Good as Fulfillment of Duty

It might strike one as odd to consider the fulfillment of duty as a good to be actively and anxiously pursued by humans as their goal in life, but for many, particularly theists, living out what one has been assigned in this life is the most noble, most gratifying experience possible. C. S. Lewis, the theologian, philosopher, and science fiction author, developed a twentieth-century alternative to the traditional definitions of sin and duty. He created a Christian worldview in which humans "owe" it to God as a duty to realize their highest potential. Sin therefore becomes self-abuse; virtue, the perfection of the self, is its own reward; and vice or viciousness, the destruction of the self, is its own punishment. Far from being an onerous task or too weighty an assignment, fulfillment of duty can, depending on one's concept of the duty, actually bring the individual constant improvement and deeper satisfaction. It should be noted that not all who subscribe to the concept of the good as duty would subscribe to Lewis's concepts of sin, virtue, and vice, but Lewis's view reveals that fulfilling our duty need not keep us from human contentment and happiness. Lewis stresses that duty is thrust upon the individual, and that he or she may commit to action on the basis of principles is as critical in assessing ethical development as the particular notion of duty involved in any version of the theory. Unlike the animals that are driven by instinct to survive, people can choose to be committed to a duty, recognize it as authoritative, embrace it, and, finally, live it out. Because such behavior is an exercise in the highest human powers, humans choosing the good life would have to make such a commitment and action.

Religious worldviews frequently adopt this version of the good and designate a god or gods as the source of the duty that humankind experiences. People in the Western traditions treat the divine being as a parental figure. As good children obey their parents, good religious adults obey the Father or Mother God. The good life is peppered with difficulties, disappointments, and, sometimes, human disasters, but, according to religious worldviews, loyalty to one's God and persistence in performing one's duty will make a virtuous life and merit a joyful one hereafter. Ethics takes on a different tone when the goal is removed from the here and now to the hereafter. When the reward and ultimate verification of the system are in the afterlife, the values must be accepted on faith in religious contexts or on authority in secular contexts. In either case, however, recognition, identification, and fulfillment of duty are treated as the greatest intellectual and emotional feats worthy of human pursuit.

The Good as Cultural Advancement

Those who are philosophically inclined to weigh the objective and stable more heavily than the subjective and transitory prefer to define the good in terms of benefit to the entire human species. Such a system recognizes the needs and desires of most members of a group. For example, the rule utilitarians judge actions according to their impact on the whole society. They consider ethically right actions that, if performed regularly, would favorably affect the group as a whole, even at considerable expense to some. The standard is the good of the majority. Because individuals learn to subordinate their own interests to those of the species, they ensure that the group will survive, even if it must be at the individual's expense. This orientation has a very strong conceptual appeal in that it eliminates from consideration of the good the perhaps eccentric or idiosyncratic tastes and preferences of some individuals and, instead, addresses only those values that clearly apply to any member.

The popularity of this ethical theory has waned in the United States since the 1960s because of the increased emphasis on the individual and the individual's right to question and even defy authority. Just as the theories that focus solely on the individual become myopic and almost exclusively subjective, theories that stress the group to the exclusion of the individual lapse into an overly objective and often rigid perspective. We cannot ignore either our individual or social natures without producing a lopsided ethical theory.

A predominant focus on the individual arises naturally in the ethical theories of younger people because in one's early and middle adult years the major goal of maturation is to separate oneself from one's family and to form one's own values. In one's older adult years, as one anticipates death, one shifts emphasis shifts to the group as one views the chain of human generations and sees the continuation of the species as an extension of oneself. Life goes on through the species.

How Free Are We to Choose?

Another story, "The Land of Certus," in Davis's text on philosophy features the inhabitants of a small country who glow red or green according to the ethical quality of their behavior.[9] One of the inhabitants, who was hosting a human visitor, explained the lights as his species' indicators of right and wrong. The human noted, for example, that when the inhabitants drank intoxicating beverages in moderation, they would glow green. However, when one inhabitant drank to excess, he glowed red, which signaled the disapproval of his fellows and prompted him to apologize. The human was impressed and not a little envious of these beings and their apparently sure system. He explained to his host that on earth there is great disagreement over which behavior is right and which is wrong, but in Certus there seemed to be no need or opportunity for disagreement because the lights provided objective criteria and eliminated messy discussions about conscience, absolutism, and utilitarianism. Later the human discovered that one of the inhabitants actually chose to disregard the lights, maintaining that the lights were unreliable and misleading, perhaps even the work of a malevolent god. He pointed out that, for example, the lights indicated that murder or theft was wrong and that regarding women as inferior to men was right. He considered the latter indication utterly wrong despite the clear green light. This inhabitant continually decided for himself and persisted in his beliefs even when he glowed the brightest red, which, of course, resulted in considerable censure and social instability. His fellow citizens were enraged at his stubbornness and subjected him to the cruelest tortures possible. When the visitor spoke out angrily against this barbaric treatment, he was rebuked by his host and commanded to look at the executioners. The visitor saw that they were all glowing green, a sure sign that what they did was ethically right. He quickly apologized to his host and removed himself from the scene.

The impact of this story on students using Davis's text is generally quite forceful. They experience an inner struggle as they consider the conflicting signals or lights (authority figures) on the one side and their feelings and intuitions (the dictates of their conscience) on the other. As long as the story is treated as a work of fiction, they feel safe in criticizing and rejecting the faulty authority, but, as we have already noted, they generally lack the ability to turn their reason and analysis on a real authority figure.

Most of us are raised with the notion that a personal conscience serves as our ethical barometer, so to speak. We are taught to consult our consciences when no authority is available and, thus, we may feel unsure of the ethical propriety of an action. On occasion, many of us hear our consciences even when we intentionally avoid consulting them. We become aware of this sixth sense that reports on the ethical quality of actions in much the same way that our sense of hearing or taste detects the qualities of sounds and foods. Our presumption that our consciences are just another sense gives them an air of objectivity and reliability which is probably not warranted. Our consciences, unlike our sense of smell, are shaped by those who train us as youngsters. The contents of one's conscience can be traced back to the authority figures who programmed it. How one is raised and what one experiences inevitably affect one's conscience. Being subjected to emotional abuse, cruelty, or insensitivity will generally not cause one to mistake blue for yellow, say, but it can significantly warp one's conscience.

If we overhaul our ethical systems, we must first recognize and examine the guides that have been instilled in each of us by our parents, teachers, religion, and society. We must then attend to our thoughts and feelings as we form a standard that we can live with emotionally and understand conceptually. How free we are to choose is a function of how free we are to trust our emotions, reasoning skills, and personalities. These create the goals and values that are genuinely ours and not simply the product of someone else's desires and worldviews.

How Free Are We to Act?

Traditional Notions of Freedom and Responsibility

If you have ever attended a moving piano recital, or if you are yourself a musician, you realize that several conditions must connect in just the right way and at the right time to produce that special effect we describe as brilliant and alive. The pianist cannot do this alone—a finely crafted and tuned instrument and an exquisite piece to perform are also necessary. Despite these requirements, we still consider the pianist's contribution pivotal and worthy of our praise and admiration. We do not focus on the piano or the piece or the hall's acoustical properties. But why? All of those elements are causes without which the performance could never happen, so why single out the pianist? The critical factor, from the human point of view, is control. We want to be more than mere "conduits of causation," as Daniel Dennett describes the phenomenon in his work *Elbow Room.*[1] The piano does not decide to participate and plays no active role whatsoever in the performance; its role is entirely passive. Likewise the piece, the hall, and so on, contribute to the performance by the way they are designed, constructed, and acted upon but not because of any effort or volition on their part. They have no control. One could just as easily applaud the laws of physics as the real cause of the performance by explaining how the piano works mechanically or even how the muscles in the pianist's hands make it possible to play the instrument. But these causes are all nonvolitional and oblivious to the event itself: only the pianist exerts the control we desire. But, traditionally, the desire to have control has been confused with the desire to have freedom, and this confusion still infects many a philosophical debate. We agonize over the issue of freedom (Could I have done otherwise?) when the real issue is control (Was I the one directing the action or behavior?).

The two issues are related because having control of one's life and actions is one of the conditions of freedom. However, we never exert complete control in any situation; for example, we are unable to control gravity or other forces that affect actions such as flying a plane or diving or building a house of cards. Therefore the issue must come down to the type or degree of control that we exert. Consider, for example, a simple choice: I go out to lunch and find I cannot decide between a chicken or beef sandwich. The locus of the choice seems definitely to be my *self:* no one else seems ready or able to determine my preference in this matter, and there is no one standing by physically restraining me or manipulating me. If I do choose the chicken sandwich, I may wonder whether my choice was a free one and whether I had enough control to make a genuine choice. External controls that influenced that simple choice were extensive: I may well not have enough money with me to buy both, and so do not have that option; I cannot ask for a half of each sandwich since the restaurant will not accommodate that choice; I am deciding under time restraints and therefore cannot thoroughly investigate all the influences on my preference; I am aware that chicken is considered the more healthful choice, but I also realize that the chicken is fried while the beef is not, and so on. All of these factors, and hundreds of others, actually influence my choice while I stand deliberating, aware only of my uncertainty about which would taste better to me today. Even if I could identify all the facets of that decision, I would not then just throw up my hands in despair and conclude that, because of the number of factors beyond my control, my choice was not my choice. Those things may all lie outside my control, but what remains in my control is what our species construes to be the critical part of the process: I experience my purchase as my preference, even if the self exerting that preference has been shaped by forces that I probably have never even detected, much less controlled. We do not need to have total control to be satisfied, but we need a certain level of control to characterize the actions as "free" or "self-directed" or "self-controlled" behavior.

Freedom is a tough metaphysical nut to crack because so much of the issue is a matter of ascertaining unrealized potentials and things that might have been. I want to be the captain of my fate, so to speak, and interpret that remark to mean that when I choose to do X, I have chosen from a field of other genuine candidates. Our belief that we are truly free springs from our intuitive experience of choosing. We make some agonizing choices from several options and we may feel uncertain right up to the actual moment of commitment. We feel that the choices we labor over and struggle with must be genuine options for us, or else the intellectually challenging and emotionally wrenching process of choosing is actually just a sham. If my choice is as necessary a result of the choosing process as corrosion is of exposure to salt and water, then my experience of choosing is a deception, and a tragic one. I would feel as though I might pursue any of the so-called choices before me when in reality I would be experiencing only the illusion of choosing, the illusion of freedom.

Why we focus so on the ability and opportunity to choose deserves attention in more spheres than merely the ethical one. Our species seems to value choice, not only as a trustworthy means of attaining the best results for ourselves but also as an intrinsically valuable exercise. Choosing is an expression of the self that we all learn to associate with autonomy and self-direction. Every child reaches a stage when, although an adult could no doubt make a better choice, the child values the right to express his or her own choice. We all want the right to direct our own lives even when our choices bring us more pain and disappointment than we would have experienced at the direction of another. We seem to be driven to discriminate, consider, and choose for ourselves. Being able to choose seems to be part of being a self. Therefore, we view any theory of how we humans function in the world that deprives us of genuine choice and threatens to minimize or cut off our choices as unsatisfactory. The large variety of such philosophical theories, all generally different versions of determinism, have provided challenging foils for competing theories on human nature but have not enjoyed wide acclaim because of their pessimistic message about human freedom.

In Davis's introduction to the issue of freedom and the problems it poses, entitled "A Little Omniscience Goes a Long Way," he presents a discussion between God and Satan concerning the control that God's omniscience seems to exert over his creatures.[2] If God knows what all creatures will choose before they actually choose it, then what genuine choice is really open to them? Are they really choosing at all, or simply playing out a role that was written before time began and could not be played out any other way? In the story, Satan arrives in heaven and announces that he wishes to speak to God about a little problem. God replies that he knows that. Satan then complains that he and the angels are displeased about God's complete knowledge of and thus control over all their behavior, to which God again replies that he knows that. And when, in exasperation, Satan points out how irritating it is that God not only runs the show but constantly reminds everyone of his omniscience, God once again replies that he, of course, knows that. In fact, God reveals that cosmic boredom is the price that he must pay for omniscience: nothing new or unexpected can ever happen to one who is omniscient.

For us humans, God's foreknowledge seems tantamount emotionally to our lack of freedom, because foreknowledge seems to negate the value of our deliberation. We create science fiction horror movies that treat time as the playing out of our decisions along a fixed path that we must travel along but cannot direct or influence, as though the course were set and we could see what the future holds for us if we could only peek or race ahead. Unless I can believe I make a contribution genuinely and freely along the way, then I become a more sophisticated piano playing a less sophisticated piano, and we are both being played by some other freer and more powerful pianist.

But the quandary I believe I am in is really only a pseudo-problem. I am treating predictability as a refutation of freedom because I have mistakenly equated freedom with lack of causation. For foreknowledge to be foreknowledge and not just foreguessing, one must have certainty that events will occur as one predicts they will. Certainty comes from accurately identifying the causes and the laws of causation. After that, predicting the inexorable result is a mere matter of extrapolation. Thinking of choosing this way seems, to most of us, rather demeaning, but what appears to lack genuine human input is actually still under our control in the ways we consider most significant.

If foreknowledge still seems to be a bar to true freedom, suppose you are standing on a very high bluff, looking down at a winding path on which two cars are traveling in opposite directions—one up the mountain, the other down. You know the terrain and are aware that the road is wide enough for only one car and you note that both cars are moving dangerously fast. You realize that, although you can see what is happening, neither driver can see the other. Neither of them anticipates the disaster that you do. If you calculate their relative positions and speed, you can say with certainty that an accident is going to happen. You have not caused it and cannot stop it, but you understand this before either driver does. By understanding how cars work and how long it takes a driver to respond, you would know that after a certain time the accident would be inevitable. That knowledge would play no part in the causal chain that led up to the wreck. Foreknowledge is really a matter of perspective; it is so called because one knows earlier than others how events are accumulating. But knowing first does not bestow on one enhanced powers or responsibilities. Sometimes to know ahead only creates greater distress at one's inability to intervene.

To define freedom as lack of causation is the first misstep in the analysis. For events to simply happen without any cause, completely randomly, does not create freedom for anyone and is truly not attractive or desirable, even to those who find predictability unpalatable. If I were to act freely under that definition, I would be just as likely to type *asdfliu* as to type the next word of this text, and then, instead of walking toward my office, I might drop to the floor and roll around or I might begin singing and then eating the paper clips. With no cause to my actions there would also be no order or pattern or purpose. In other words, random behavior is senseless behavior, not behavior that I would call mine, and definitely not what we envision when we think of freedom. By freedom, what we really mean is behavior that is caused, but caused by us. We want our actions to proceed from us in such a way that we can accurately be described as the causes of the action or behavior. Again, I need not be the only causal factor for the action to flow from me, but I must be the most significant, in human terms, among the many causes.

Now we see why the pianist is singled out from among the many causes that created the concert. We recognize the pianist's contribution as the uniquely human, dynamic component. The quality of the composition and the workings of the piano are, of course, essential as well, but the component that combines all those factors in this recital is the pianist. The pianist's active role is revered and admired because he or she has focused his or her talent, effort, and artistic genius—what we recognize as distinctly human contributions—to create this particular performance. If someone pointed out that the pianist could never have performed so well had the strings on the piano been broken or the soundboard warped, we would acknowledge the accuracy of the observation but would probably wonder at the triviality of that truth. The influence of external forces does not dwarf the artist's contribution, because we recognize this effect in our assessment of human performance.

If the direction on my part is truly on my part, then I can legitimately claim and describe the performance as directed by my hand despite the vast number of other causes that affected me throughout its creation. Far from being a mere puppet, I am more like the driver of a car. I cannot radically change its physical structure or its capabilities (I cannot, for example, expect a car to do what a microwave oven does), but I can direct which of the possible courses it will take and how many of its capabilities will be exercised and when. So, predictability becomes more and more possible, not because I am less and less free to act, but rather because the outside forces are constant, fairly obvious, and easy to identify, and my nature, as an emerging and growing identity, becomes more set over time and takes on a more permanent and identifiable character. That most of us can predict whether a loved one would prefer apple pie or coconut cake for dessert does not in any way negate that person's freedom to choose one or the other. We know the person well, and therefore can often predict what the person will prefer; we do not cause his or her actions, we simply understand the personality of the chooser. Predictability need not threaten our ability to choose at all. If a person were completely unpredictable, we would be concerned that he or she lacked a stable personality. We would not consider such a person to be more free but scattered and without a strong sense of self.

We become selves slowly, over a lifetime, as our choices build on one another and as patterns develop. We experience the self as a constant, unchanging thread running through all our thoughts and actions over a lifetime, but that self is built up out of all of the experiences and choices that we have faced and negotiated up to the moment. It evolves, albeit gradually, with each passing day. We describe this series of minuscule changes as the process of life—the maturation process—and we recognize that when our personalities become sufficiently set and stable, by whatever standard we may choose as our marker, then we are considered adults and our actions are viewed as truly our own.

Our core comes into existence only through millions of sequences of conflict-deliberation-choice-resolution. For individuals to act in the ethical sphere, the self must have sufficiently developed so that we can call it responsible for its behavior. Pinpointing exactly what is conclusive evidence of sufficient development is no mean feat. On the surface, after we reach a particular chronological age, we all look like adults and therefore we assume that our individual selves are, likewise, more or less mature. Unfortunately appearances can be quite deceptive. To evaluate how good a piano is one must play it, not simply look at it, because a piano's excellence is revealed only through the playing of it. The self's excellence is revealed only through its exercise of its major powers or functions: choosing from among the myriad possible behaviors open to the individual and then guiding the person through that maze of activity. What people choose to do with their lives and how they act on those choices reveals how developed their senses of self really are. Choices are a logical focal point of our analysis of the self because choices reveal the values that are embraced by the self, and the values reveal our axioms, logical rules, and theorems, which compose the core of the ethical being. Assessing an individual's ethical responsibility for any act requires evaluating the extent to which the individual has been able to choose and direct his or her behavior. Those conditions that restrain the individual's choice can be properly said to limit his or her responsibility.

This message is difficult for many people to accept because it seems to create a loophole for adults to escape responsibility for their actions. An old Monty Python comedy sketch portrayed the murder of a prominent Anglican bishop. When the Church Squad investigating the crime pray for guidance in identifying the murderer, a huge hand emerges from a cloud and points at a bystander. The church members confront the man and ask if he did, in fact, murder the bishop. He confesses that he did, but claims that society is actually to blame for the crime. They agree, release him, and announce that they will go out and arrest society. What most find unsettling about this is the ambiguity created when the responsibility is shifted from me to the people who have shaped my character and contributed to the person that I now am. They number in the thousands, and many are now so removed from me and my life that they might no longer even remember who I am. It is, of course, much simpler and more intuitively satisfying if we deem the man holding the smoking gun responsible rather than his long-deceased younger brother who always ridiculed him and destroyed his self-esteem. To acknowledge that our actions are affected so significantly by others is a mere intellectual concession to the fact that we are complex beings and that we retain deep inside our consciousness the remnants of past experiences and relationships. But to assign ethical responsibility to those who have exerted such influence is impractical for obvious reasons and also risky from a logical point of view: can I pinpoint and identify accurately the forces that have shaped my temperament? Can I know just who did what to me and what impact they had? And although this move absolves me of some of the responsibility for what I have done in this world, what about the role I have played in the development of others and of their behavior? I would literally become my brother's keeper and I would also find myself being held responsible for others' actions. Of course, in the end, we believe that someone must be responsible. So, we keep changing our methods of pinpointing influences on human choice in the hope of being more thorough and accurate in identifying the true cause of human behavior, but as we move farther from the actual agent we encounter a seemingly endless array of suspects, all of whom have exerted some influence, but none of whom seem to be any more in control than we are ourselves. There seems to be no ready solution to the problem of identifying the source of ethical liability. If we do relinquish blameworthiness, we end with the most disturbing question: if we are not responsible for our actions, then who is?

Like freedom, responsibility is a difficult concept to define because it describes at least two extremely different concepts: physical causation and ethical liability. If I am carrying a large punch bowl filled to the very top with punch and, as I walk slowly and carefully across the room, I trip over a shoe carelessly left on the floor, one can say that the shoe was responsible for the accident, in that it was the physical cause of my accident. However, it would be a most peculiar use of the term to say that the shoe was responsible in the sense of being ethically liable. The shoe bears no fault or blameworthiness despite its principal role in the mishap. Likewise, if the metal door handle at my parents' beach cottage comes loose and they explain that rust was responsible for the disintegration of the handle, they would certainly not then blame the rust or evaluate its "behavior" as in any way ethically inappropriate. Rust simply does what rust does, and my parents' use of the term *responsible* would clearly indicate mere physical causation and with no ethical overtones. On the other hand, when a child is constantly mistreated by his parents, either through emotional or physical abuse, and we learn that the child later became a juvenile prostitute or drug pusher, we will frequently speak as though the parents are responsible, even though they may know nothing about the child's situation. They did not introduce the child to prostitution and may have never used drugs themselves, and they may be able to honestly say that they would never have intended such a career for their offspring. By holding the parents responsible, we are not identifying them as the physical cause of their child's situation, but rather we are calling them ethically liable: the parents' mistreatment of the child affected him in such a negative way that he was driven to those acts. We acknowledge that the true blameworthiness lies with the parents, not the child. The difference between the physical causation and ethical liability needs to be borne in mind, otherwise identifying the physical causes will be interpreted as deflecting ethical liability, when, in fact, the two are separate. Questions about why something has happened can lead to unexpected responses. A friend of mine who teaches philosophy was asked by a student, "Dr. Walker, why did you give me a grade of 'F' on this assignment?" And my friend astutely replied: "Because that's the lowest grade they'll let me give."

As do our concerns about the control we exert over our actions, our concerns about our responsibility for our actions deal more with the types of responsibility than with whether we are ever really solely responsible for our actions. We have developed a sense of the extent to which we must be in control and responsible in order to declare ourselves the actual agents of our actions and the ones responsible for what has transpired. In order to be responsible in the sense of being ethically liable for an action, certain conditions, particularly knowledge and freedom, must be in place to ensure that individuals can assert themselves and own their choices and actions.

Intellectual, Emotional, and Psychological Factors

Milton Gonsalves, in his revision of *Fagothey's Right and Reason*, examines what he terms "modifiers of responsibility," conditions that represent degrees of impairment of our ability to choose, act on those choices, and therefore be responsible for our behavior.[3] These conditions cause (in the purely physical sense) us to be either more or less limited or free in our choices and actions. Therefore, the conditions actually regulate our capacity for ethical behavior and our willingness to act ethically. We, in turn, can minimize the debilitating effects on us through our own efforts. The five major modifiers, with a number of minor factors, which represent variations on the major themes, are ignorance, strong emotion, fear, force, and habit.

Ignorance

Ignorance is generally a selectively exercised function that we all indulge in, or are victimized by, at one time or another; it exists in varying degrees, sometimes exercised through our own fault, sometimes through the fault of no one, sometimes restricted to certain sensitive issues, sometimes more the rule than the exception. In other words, as long as we are finite, we will all suffer from some ignorance, but this does not condemn us to total stupidity and lack of awareness. Ignorance is sometimes vincible, sometimes (but rarely) totally invincible.

Vincible ignorance is ignorance that we can recognize, effectively confront, and overcome: information is available to fill in the gaps and enable us to anticipate the reactions, implications, and effects of our behavior and therefore make a reasonable ethical choice. In wrestling with ethical dilemmas, an often critical consideration is the results of each course of action: how would each affect a person and those around him or her? What one ought to do requires considering many factors in the ethical dilemma: if I consider, for example, the possible ethical responsibility I may bear for the homeless or the starving in my neighborhood, I must first attempt to understand the causes and nature of the problem, the possible means of solving the problem, and the realistic ideas about the impact that I might be able to make. And if I really would simply rather not know about the problem and therefore attempt to avoid ethical responsibility, I can always opt for ignorance as a way out of the dilemma. As long as I can avoid knowing how bad the homelessness and hunger really are and what I might do to help, I can forestall the need to act. This selective, voluntarily exercised ignorance is vincible because I could easily find out all that I would really need to know to make an informed decision about what role, if any, I should play in solving this monumental social problem. It should be noted that acquiring information and thereby eliminating ignorance does not immediately create in me an ethical demand to act. In this example, I may sincerely decide, after studying the problem, that the only means to effectively relieve the problem would be to commit substantial time or money to the agencies that feed the hungry and shelter the homeless. I may further decide that, although this is a serious problem and in great need of volunteers and monetary contributions, I am currently incapable, because of other obligations, of committing myself to the extent necessary. In that case, I would need to accept my analysis of the situation (assuming that I have been honest, informed, and sincere), recognize my limits, and acknowledge that I would be acting in a responsible manner to simply not act at this time, despite the fact that I would not be helping the homeless or starving. Of course, the conclusion that I present above as a possible choice is not the only possible conclusion: I may decide that (*a*) the situation is so serious that I should offer any effective help that I can; (*b*) the situation can truly be bettered through short-term volunteer efforts that I could offer now, despite my obligations, and; therefore, (*c*) that I ought to offer my services and help relieve some of the suffering. No two people will answer the question "Am I ethically obliged to help?" the same way. What we can and must do, assuming we have a genuine desire to make effective decisions about ethical duty, is become informed and sincerely use the information to decide our action. Also, if we are going to make our own decisions in a responsible manner, we must respect others' decisions about their ethical duties, even if we would have decided otherwise. Individual freedom necessarily implies that we will, at times, differ widely in our choices. If one feels that another's decision is based on ignorance or, perhaps, faulty information or reasoning, then one may sincerely and respectfully offer information, but the browbeating and manipulating that each of us has, at one time or another, experienced at the hands of those who disagreed with us is not appropriate. The keys to ethical freedom are open-mindedness, sincerity, and the willingness to grant others the same freedom.

In addition to vincible ignorance, there is also invincible ignorance, the inevitable result of our finitude, and, unfortunately, a barrier to total certainty in ethical matters. In human affairs, where people's perceived needs, desires, wants, and so on, are at stake, I can make certain educated guesses about the outcome of my or others' behaviors. But all of us at times make errors in predicting how others feel or how they might respond. In fact, at times we even predict incorrectly our own reactions: what we thought we would appreciate or approve of, we find ourselves displeased by or even offended by, despite our careful and deliberate analysis. This means that infallibility in the ethical sphere is not an option for us: in ethical matters, like all other matters, we have some certainty, but there is also much room for error and miscalculation. Errors will happen sufficiently often to remind us that we are merely human. Our responsibility is almost never complete (we cannot attain total knowledge for our decision-making), but our responsibility is not dependent on our being omniscient: it is a function of how much vincible ignorance we eliminate and how sincerely and carefully we analyze our dilemmas in light of the best information available to us.

Strong Emotion

Strong emotion limits our responsibility by overwhelming us or blinding us to what our reason dictates. Because of our human nature, some situations will provoke strong, perhaps even irresistible, urges to react. We call it a crime of passion, for example, when a person discovers his or her spouse in the arms of another lover and, in a moment of fury, kills the spouse or the spouse's lover. We perceive some situations to be so volatile that it is unrealistic to expect a person to make calm decisions. We say "There but for the grace of God go I" and treat individuals in that situation as essentially at the mercy of forces beyond their control. We may say that the action is only partially excused, but even then we realistically acknowledge that the control of people in that situation has been seriously impaired, despite their best intentions or desire to remain rational. Therefore in emotional life, which may be attended by emotional upheaval or passionate force, we can expect the individual's capacity to reason and therefore to choose wisely and thoughtfully to be limited. The debilitation may not be so great as to destroy the individual's responsibility entirely, but it can and will hinder his or her ethical effectiveness and must be recognized as a prominent influence.

Of course, strong emotions can also be cultivated and nursed and encouraged so that their effects begin to more closely resemble planned or intended responses rather than unexpected eruptions. If you work yourself into a frenzy while knowing that you are a person who has a hair-trigger temper, then you are responsible for having set off your temper yourself by catering to it and encouraging it. In cases such as this, one is responsible because one has assumed ethical liability. Hiding behind overwhelming emotion is just a sham. Nursing a grudge against another and harboring anger and ill-will create the perfect medium for cultivating an explosive temper. Becoming a mature adult entails developing the patience and self-control to rein in one's temper: childish tantrums do not belong in the repertoire of adult behavior. Feeling deeply is perfectly appropriate for adults, but exhibiting wildly fluctuating and out-of-control behavior is clearly not the mark of a disciplined, well-developed self.

Fear

Fear is the most misunderstood of the factors that inhibit our ability to choose, because many misinterpret it to be the sort of fear experienced by one being kidnapped or coerced into some horrible action, when, actually, the fear is much more mundane. Those who fashion their own ethical system but then lose their nerve because parents, friends, bosses, and so on will disapprove of their system are acting out of fear. Those who simply cannot consider changing careers or giving up a destructive relationship because they cannot bear to give up the comfort of the familiar or the luxuries that the current arrangement or paycheck affords are acting out of fear. The addict who keeps promising to stop tomorrow but can never quite face life without drugs or alcohol is acting out of fear. It is not the things that are causing us to act: it is fear of life without these things that drives us, and our response to the fear is itself a choice. Because we are more afraid of the pain or discomfort of losing these things than we are of the price we pay for them, we settle for a less than honest, less than fulfilling life.

Are we responsible for this fear? We are not responsible for its existence, because we cannot control the eruption of such feelings, but when we choose to give in to fear and let it have its way over us, then—at the moment we choose to let it control our behavior and limit our lives—we are the agents, and we are ethically liable for the lifestyle we embrace. The overwhelming success of Twelve-Step programs in treating addictions attests to one's power to face the fear head on—with the help and support of other addicts—and, so, to reclaim autonomy in one's own life.

Force

Force is frequently confused with fear, described above, because those who are addicted or overly attached to unhealthy habits or lifestyles often describe themselves as forced into these habits against their wills. This is not true force, because there is still an opportunity to resist effectively. Responding to threats, likewise, is really more properly an issue of fear than one of force. Actual physical force used against me to coerce me to act in a particular way produces involuntary action and cannot really remove my ability to will otherwise. I am simply prevented from responding to my will. If physical force is applied, my responsibility is modified only by my resistance to the force. If I offer no resistance but act as directed, whether or not I have been an active accomplice is a genuine issue. If I have given consent, then I am, of course, responsible for my actions and cannot claim that I was forced. Patty Hearst, the heiress who was kidnapped and held captive for many months, faced a tremendous hurdle in her defense against charges of bank robbery when she claimed her role was the result of force, though film footage of the crime showed her armed and waving the gun around while appearing calm and almost cocky about her actions. Genuine force will remove my responsibility for my actions, but I must actively resist (although the degree of resistance required is difficult to decide). I cannot count mere emotional pressure or manipulation as force.

Habit

Habit can be an insidious foe, because it is practically invisible to the individual caught in it. Habit is a pattern of behavior that has been repeated so many times that it becomes ingrained, requiring no conscious effort to trigger or play out. Most habits are relatively harmless: putting one's left shoe on first, eating food quickly or slowly, taking the stairs two at a time, and so on. However, the role of habit is significant when examining ethical behavior because habitual acts by definition lie outside our awareness and control. Being exclusively a creature of habit means being a stagnant creature that does not examine, question, or rethink its patterns of behavior. Even the most innocuous unconscious patterns of behavior can blind us and direct our attention and behavior along paths that are no longer appropriate or that no longer work with our more mature and consciously chosen worldviews. We need to become more conscious beings, not less conscious.

The Role of Motives in Ethical Action

The intellectual facets of good motives have been emphasized thus far because reason can readily redirect and manipulate them but a plan to extensively alter human behavior may still entail a change of heart. Creating a significantly different attitude in the populace constitutes a major challenge, of course, but, as we have seen, attempts to bypass the essential attitude shift by substituting the carrot and the stick proves useless. For permanent, consistent, and reliable behavioral changes, attitudes must be addressed. Freedom to act can be as effectively restricted by one's own attitudes as by those of others. Luckily, attitudes depend on knowledge, therefore, education can influence human attitudes and behavior.

In Morton Hunt's studies, reported in *The Compassionate Beast*, psychologists and sociologists examined compassionate behavior and questioned whether, indeed, human beings are the only species that exhibits what we would define as compassionate acts or altruistic behavior. Hunt's conclusions about their results are important to our discussion because he notes that if we judge altruism merely on behavior, and not the motive behind it, then many other species seem to exhibit altruistic behavior—behavior in which the good of another is placed before the good of the actor, with no expectation on the actor's part of any reward. Hunt cites certain species of birds, including robins, thrushes, and titmice, that, through instinct, sing a warning song when a predator is nearby. The melody varies to warn the rest of their kind whether the menace is approaching by air or on the ground. While the others flee, the altruistic bird leaves itself vulnerable by not hiding, by actually crying out and calling attention to itself. Hunt further notes that these birds, when raised apart from others of their kind, would, when a predator approached, sound the danger signal, even if there were no others nearby to be warned. The behavior therefore seems to be instinctive and not learned from other birds, and also was clearly not the result of imitating other birds.[4] Therefore, given the obvious helpful nature of such actions, why might we still refrain from calling these birds altruistic or compassionate? Hunt identifies the characteristic that we humans think of as the ultimate criterion of ethical behavior: the behavior must not only correspond to the right thing to do, but it must be performed for particular reasons and performed intentionally.[5] For humans, it is not only the result of the behavior that indicates its ethical worth. The right motive and the ability to have acted otherwise are implicit but powerful components in the analysis.

In the movie *A Clockwork Orange* a man committed unspeakable acts of cruelty and violence. In place of customary punishment, he was reprogrammed (brainwashed) so that any urge to repeat the act would cause him overwhelming sickness or pain. Did his reformed behavior indicate that he was acting ethically? Most people would say no, and add that the man could no longer act in an ethical manner simply because he could no longer genuinely choose how he might act. To others his behavior would appear voluntary and indistinguishable from self-directed, purposeful restraint, but it would actually be more closely akin to the robin's warning than virtuous human behavior. He clearly did not intend to do the right thing. He simply was incapable of doing the wrong thing.

I once sat through an afternoon of presentations by Florida State University graduate students on the synopses of their master's theses. The students covered the entire spectrum of possible topics in the natural sciences, but only one really held my attention. This student had studied the fire ant, a prevalent pest in Florida. He had observed that minutes after a fire ant dies in the colony two other ants leave their work, pick up the dead ant, carry it to the edge of the colony, leave the body, and return to their work. When another ant dies, two different ants remove the dead body. All ants that died in the colony were carried to the same place. If you merely observed the behavior and did not have other knowledge about ants, you might conclude that the ants exhibited intelligent and even caring behavior. For example, when a dog or a raccoon is killed on the road, you do not see others of its kind carry it away. However, the ants behaved very much as humans do when a member of the group dies. One might even have guessed that they could have recognized the deceased and might even have been saddened by its death. If the student's study had stopped there, I would have been convinced that ants experience and express empathy or sympathy that exceeded any I had ever seen in the animal kingdom below human beings. But this enterprising biology student pressed his study further and shattered my misconception. He discovered what signaled the other ants that one of their company had died (a chemical produced by the body's decomposition) and then squirted some of the chemical on a live ant. After several minutes, two ants picked up the live ant, disregarding its flailing legs, dutifully carried it to the edge of the colony, and dropped it on the pile of dead ants. The two carriers and the "corpse" then all returned to work until the next two ants picked up the scent. The ant was carried out and crawled back until the chemical finally wore off. What appeared to be compassionate behavior was revealed to be rigidly mechanical and thoughtless. The fire ants had no motive and no intention—merely instinct.

How the act appears is frequently misleading. When we read certain motives into actions and actors, we may misread what is happening. It is not the mere quality of the behavior toward another or the good that may accrue to the beneficiary that distinguishes genuinely altruistic acts: the actor's motive and intention are both critical to identifying altruistic behavior.

Hunt wisely comments on the false dichotomy that many set up between truly altruistic acts—those acts in which the actor not only acts for another, but acts solely for that other, perhaps even to the detriment of his or her own interests—and selfish acts, in which the actor may help others, and be genuinely motivated and intend to do so, but also reap certain benefits. Hunt suggests that we can preserve the real essence of the term altruistic if we acknowledge that performing acts that help both the other and oneself should be categorized as genuinely *altruistic* so long as one would have performed them for the other even if there had not been any benefit for oneself. In other words, we need not be driven to acts of extreme self-deprivation to earn the title of altruist; the most important factor is the proper motive, not the outcome. Extending oneself for the benefit of others is sufficient to establish one's action as an altruistic one.

Motive also colors the ethical character of actions. Ethical actions involve more than proper judgments, they involve proper desires. Intentions are often confused with motives, although they are distinctly different. In a criminal case, for example, the prosecution is required to prove whether the act was intentional (sometimes broadly construed to include the results of inexcusable neglect), but need never say or prove anything about the motive. The intention of an action refers to the actor's commitment to perform the act, whereas the motive is whatever reason the actor may have entertained for performing the action. Since the number of possible motives for any action is (at least theoretically) infinite, in view of the range of reasonable and unreasonable beliefs a person may entertain at any time, it would be impossible to ever convict anyone if the prosecutor were required to dig out and argue the worth of a defendant's motives. However, unlike criminal cases, ethically correct behavior seems to be characterized by certain motives—most commonly, a desire to do what is right.

Suppose, for example, that Person A has decided to murder Person B and plans his moves, buys a gun and ammunition, and plants himself in a spot by which Person B is bound to pass at the end of the day. Assume further that, exactly when Person B does pass by, among many people on the sidewalk, Person C, behind Person B, suddenly goes berserk and fires indiscriminately into the crowd. Person A pulls the trigger at that moment, intending to kill B, but hits C by accident, shooting the gun out of his hand without seriously injuring him, putting an end to C's senseless killing spree. Person A is, of course, praised by the crowd and the media for his quick response in the emergency and for saving countless lives. But was Person A really a hero? Was he acting ethically? To answer that question, several other questions need to be addressed.

1. Is it ever ethically correct to injure (and risk even killing) one person to save several others?
2. If injuring one to save others is ethically correct, then what will reveal the ethical quality of the action? (Consider, for example, how certain you must be that the others will be seriously injured or killed, how direct a cause the first individual is of the others' pain or injury, or what the motive of the first person might be.) In the example above, the role of Person C is obvious, direct, and immediate. He is not removed and acting indirectly—he is an immediate threat to everyone around him and injures as many as he can until he is stopped. His intention and motive are not known, but it is not C's motives we are concerned with here, but rather those of the person who intervenes to stop C, either intentionally or unintentionally.
3. Considering Person A's motive, would you characterize A's action as ethical? Do you find yourself focusing on the motive or the outcome of the action? Does the motive count despite the outcome, or does the outcome count despite the motive?

Many philosophers have addressed the issue of motives in ethics and have concluded that motive does count. For many, motive is the essential ingredient. I cannot often control the outcomes of my actions and decisions when others are also acting but I can control when I choose to act on my motivations.

Doing the right thing for the wrong reason and doing the wrong thing for the right reason both miss the mark, but which you consider the most offensive ethically will reveal which factor you consider most important, motive or outcome.

Many traditional philosophers and theologians have considered the problem of pursuing the right behavior for the wrong reason and have concluded that the doing is what is essential, and that the reasons behind it are merely secondary, if important at all. Their reasons for this conclusion flow from their philosophies of human nature and their concern that the measure of ethical behavior should remain how we treat one another, which emphasizes the behavior rather than the motivation.

These thinkers have acknowledged that the danger in determining what is ethically right by the motives of the actor is that no one ever acts with completely pure motives. We are all more or less flawed, ethically, despite our best efforts. It is also very difficult to assess just exactly how pure one's intentions are and exactly which of the many motives was the most prominent. Determining the ethical value of an action would be merely a rough approximation at best. In addition to properly identifying the motives, people differ in their ability to comprehend and reflect. We become socialized and learn correct habits initially by rote, years before we can consciously appreciate them (some seem never to move beyond the habit stage, as Aristotle recognized). If we stress the individual's motives rather than his or her actions, then most of us will look ethically suspect much of the time, and others of us will lose the only ethical anchor we have ever had: good habits. After all, all of us have wanted at times to inflict real damage on that driver who gleefully cuts us off or that neighbor whose dog has dug up our flowers again. We have not, of course—we have restrained ourselves—but often it is not because we really believe that it is better to hold back: we just do not want a jail term and its stigma. We are not responding to noble motives much of the time.

Before you decide to abandon motives altogether as the best indicator of ethical correctness, however, return to Persons A, B, and C. Person A has just shot the gun out of Person C's hand, ending his reckless injuring of others, and everyone has gathered around to congratulate A on his quick thinking and great courage. If his motives do not count, and the outcome of the behavior really determines the ethical character of his actions, then Person A was merely lucky, because—although not to his credit—his behavior, which would have been ethically wrong, had he been successful, was transformed into ethically praiseworthy behavior. He was transformed into a hero.

Many feel uncomfortable placing the ethical indicators outside the actor (in the results of his or her behavior), because, although our motives may be imperfect, we often exert very little control on the situations around us, and to place our ethical character in the hands of others seems to take away our sense of ethical autonomy. I cannot know if I acted in an ethically correct manner until the the final score is tallied. Suppose, for example, that Person A truly cares for and appreciates Person B, so much so that A plans a surprise party to congratulate B on his recent career change. Person A carefully plans the surprise, invites B's closest friends, and they all wait in B's dark apartment for his return from work. Unbeknownst to Person A, Person B has been struggling with great stress— both physical and emotional—in his career. Today Person B has been experiencing chest pains while he organized his new offices. As Person B enters his apartment, everyone screams "Surprise!" and, because of the shock and stress on his heart, Person B drops dead. If we now identify the cause of Person B's demise, the most obvious candidate would be that last shock administered through Person A's premeditated actions in organizing the party. The outcome, the death of Person B, could not have been achieved more efficiently if A had shot him. One could even imagine an Alfred Hitchcock thriller in which Person A would kill Person B by the same method. But, in the example, Person A did not know that Person B was having heart trouble and did not intend to kill Person B, and that makes all the difference. The fact of Person B's death cannot be judged until we understand why it happened, and that is what motives reveal.

So we have come full circle. Judging by the outcome only is unsatisfactory, because we desire to place ethical responsibility in the individual and not the conglomerate of actors and circumstances that converge in any action. But motives alone do not seem to satisfy our need to consider what we do as well as why we do it. After all, as the old saying goes, the road to hell is paved with good intentions. Meaning well is commendable, but well-intentioned destruction is still destruction, so we seem to need to compromise. One solution is to combine good motives with sufficient knowledge to make the motives effective.

Is it enough to say you meant well? Generally, no. If a friend has serious and complicated legal difficulties and I offer legal advice that she follows and that leads her into even more serious entanglements, I cannot absolve myself of responsibility merely by claiming that I meant well. That will prove a lame defense if she brings a malpractice action against me. I must do more than mean well: I must act responsibly, and that requires that I educate myself about my limitations. Caring for my friend effectively requires that I acknowledge my limitations and then either get the information to correct my deficient understanding of the issue or help my friend by researching the available resources and referring her to an attorney who can handle the matter effectively. I need not know it all, but I may not act (at least ethically) if I lack legal expertise and know, or should know, that. Thus self-knowledge becomes crucial. It is not enough to mean well but act stupidly and carelessly any more than it is praiseworthy to intend to hurt someone but create a positive effect because of unforeseen circumstances. Both elements work in tandem: responsible exercise of knowledge and good motives can create ethically good behavior, but, when either is missing, it leads to a lopsided version of morality.

In conclusion, how free we are to act is a function of several factors, some of which we control and others of which we can at best hope to recognize and mitigate through planning and effort. We can act with greater freedom if we are willing to learn about the forces that shape our motives and our ability to anticipate the likely consequences of the actions open to us.

What Difference Does Ethics Make?

Why Be Ethical?

Over two thousand years ago, Socrates declared that the unexamined life is not worth living. It is easy to hear those words as mere platitude, but Socrates was attempting to reveal a fact of life and human temperament. We are conscious, thinking beings, and we cannot live life superficially, oblivious to its meaning and its direction. The late Brandeis University psychologist Abraham Maslow reiterated the sentiments of Socrates and praised the early Greeks for their astute observations about human nature and the conditions necessary for mental health and stability.

> "Plato's words still hold," he once told an interviewer. The man who lives by "ultimate value[s] . . . stands in the sunlight and sees the real world." Maslow came to believe that the happiest individuals "are ordinarily concerned with the basic issues and eternal questions of the type that we have learned to call philosophical or ethical."[1]

Carl Jung praised the therapeutic effects of maintaining a healthy ethical-intuitive balance and "frequently warned that to privately 'cherish secrets and to restrain emotions are psychic misdemeanors for which nature finally visits us with sickness.'"[2]

The simple, direct answer to the question "Why be ethical?" can be found by observing that those who are ethical tend to lead healthier (both physically and psychologically), more emotionally satisfying lives. We need to move beyond the negative, destructive

concept of humanity as base and evil and of ethics as mysterious and self-negating to create ethical systems worthy of our
dedication and commitment. Doing what is ethically right actually uplifts a person and realizes a person's true potential. One
becomes vested in doing what is right because it is plainly in
one's best interest. Rather than being a sacrificial, difficult and
onerous task, the ethical act is, by definition, the desirable, fulfilling, and beneficial. Being ethical turns out to be the right
thing to do, not only (or even chiefly) because it promotes
social stability and order and satisfies the rule makers, but
because it makes each actor healthier and more satisfied. In
the introduction to this book, the observation was made that
ethics is, in part, what makes us tick. This is more than a mere
aphorism. Even science, the twentieth century's predominant
authority, is beginning to rediscover the link between psychological health and wholeness and humans' ethical dimension.

> Consider the resident psychiatrist at a Midwestern hospi-
> tal who encourages patients to end each day by
> meditating briefly on how honestly they have behaved
> during the past twenty-four hours. Or the New York City
> drug counselor who encourages a recovering cocaine
> addict to make a list of all the people he has harmed, for
> the purpose of making amends. . . . Statistically this grow-
> ing reliance on traditional ethical and spiritual values
> reveals itself in collective attitudes which would have been
> considered unthinkable less than a decade ago. A recent
> national survey of 425 practicing psychologists, marriage
> and family counselors, psychiatrists, and social workers, is
> revealing. Queried on what they believed to be the essen-
> tial requirements for mental health, 96 percent stressed
> the importance of patients becoming more "open, gen-
> uine, and honest." 100 percent agreed on the importance
> of "assuming responsibility for one's actions," 99 percent
> on "increasing one's capacity for self-control," . . . and a
> remarkable 96 percent on "acquiring an awareness of
> inner potential and the capacity to grow."[3]

These ethical dimensions and those cited in most works on
the resurgence of ethical therapy are the personally guided
and genuinely embraced varieties, bearing no resemblance to

the pseudo-ethical systems of conformity and blind acceptance that most people have experienced firsthand and know all too well. The old intimidating approach to the transmission of ethical values coupled with unintelligible belief systems probably prevented even professionals in the health care fields from fully recognizing the ethical dimension of mental health. Many psychologists and others trained to treat people with psychological disorders came reluctantly to the conclusion that mental health and ethical wellness were strongly linked. Two men's battles with the monumental problem of alcohol addiction revealed that a holistic approach, addressing both its psychological and ethical dimensions, was needed. Their realizations and efforts resulted in the founding of Alcoholics Anonymous:

> Perhaps the most obvious example [of ethical therapy] is in the area of treating alcohol, drug, and other addictive behaviors where conventional psychoanalysis and behaviorism are rapidly conceding defeat to the so-called "anonymous" programs, which emphasize recovery through the cultivation of ethical values and inner guidance. Inspired by the original Alcoholics Anonymous, there is now a Narcotics Anonymous, a Gamblers Anonymous, an Overeaters Anonymous, and most recently a Cocaine Anonymous. Total participation is difficult to estimate, though A.A. conservatively estimates its membership alone at "well over one million." When combined with sister organizations . . . such as Adult Children of Alcoholics and Al-Anon, the ethically oriented anonymous self-help programs currently constitute the single largest treatment program in American life.[4]

Steps Four and Five of the Twelve-Step Program call upon the addicted person to make a "searching and fearless moral inventory" and to admit "the exact nature of (his or her) wrongs."[5] The first medicine prescribed is an analysis of one's ethical state and an acknowledgment of one's condition. For the A.A. member, the unexamined life can no longer be tolerated.

But for addict and nonaddict alike examining life immediately produces a most disturbing realization: we humans are mortal. Our lives, even the longest of them, may span at best a century, and accidents and illnesses rob many of even half that time. Death eventually claims us all, the rich and the poor, the educated and uneducated alike. As far as we know, we humans are the only species that contemplates its own death. Our awareness of our mortality is reflected in every dimension of our social lives: for example, our preoccupation with looking young (even when we have long passed our youth), our mid-life crises, and the desire to leave behind children through whom we can "live on." When you do not know for sure what awaits you after this earthly existence, the need to understand the meaning and purpose of our brief time here becomes a consuming quest, more urgent as we hear the minutes of our limited time ticking away, forever lost to us.

Humans have persisted in examining and pondering the purpose behind their existence ever since the first self-conscious being appeared on the planet. Each generation experiences the question of the purpose of life and must answer it for itself in its own context. We face the crisis on two levels, as members of a species and as individuals. What makes life worthwhile? Some common themes and observations crop up, generation after generation, but this question must be faced by every person separately and must ultimately be grappled with on the individual level. Why am I here? What difference does one person make?

The Worth of One Person

> The first dilemma, in a word, is that we have no particular place to go. The species lacks any goal external to its own biological nature. It could be that in the next hundred years humankind will thread the needles of technology and politics, solve the energy and materials crises, avert nuclear war, and control reproduction. The world can at least hope for a stable ecosystem and a well-nourished population. But what then? Educated people everywhere like to believe that beyond material needs lie fulfillment and the realization of individual potential. But what is fulfillment, and to what ends may potential be realized?[6]

We spend much of our lives learning to successfully interact—to get along—with others, and we rate ourselves and our success over a lifetime in terms of how we measure up to others, usually by their standards. The social dimension is, of course, a vital part of human existence and provides us with the emotional support and nurturing that every person seeks. But, in the end, our individual selves must count if life is to have a purpose. I was born alone and will die alone. It is of little consequence to me as I ponder the question of my purpose in living that, somewhere in another part of the world, scientists are discovering the cure for cancer or another great child prodigy is blossoming: my life needs to count for something—I need to count for something. That other members of my species are making monumental contributions of their own does nothing to explain my place here. I feel a need to be more than an appendage to others. Furthermore, as mid-life approaches, one often realizes that one may have served as a perfect receptacle for others' ideas and values, but may have not contributed to the human experience anything of oneself.

How I lived and how I should have lived are the only issues that really count when I look back and take stock of my time here. Unlike an understanding of computers or my VCR, which I can leave to others to work out and apply for me, an understanding of how my life should have been lived and how I ought to have spent my time is essential for me and for every person who faces the question of his or her purpose in life. I will have little satisfaction in knowing that I successfully learned others' ideas and followed their system, even if I did it better than anyone else did. Like Sisyphus, I am given (at least as far as I know) one life, and I can either join the game as a genuine player or I can be content to be the pawn of others and, so, experience only the values that they allow and dictate.

Emerson, in his essay entitled "Self-Reliance," addressed the problem of reconciling the need for others with the need to be a genuine self and an individual and concluded that, although society seems to seek conformity from its members, conformity is actually destructive to a group, condemning it to stagnate in its past values and ideas. Groups do not make original leaps forward—individuals do and, thereby, enable a group to slowly forge ahead. But the welfare of the group truly lies at the mercy of the genius and strength of the individuals who compose it: it is the individual who acts as the catalyst for change.

> Your genuine action will explain itself and will explain your other genuine actions. Your conformity explains nothing. Act singly, and what you have already done singly will justify you now. . . . Let us affront and reprimand the smooth mediocrity and squalid contentment of the times, and hurl in the face of custom and trade and office, the fact which is the upshot of all history, that there is a great responsible Thinker and Actor moving wherever moves a man; that a true man belongs to no other time or place, but is the centre of things. Where he is, there is nature. He measures you and all men and events. . . . A man Caesar is born, and for ages after we have a Roman Empire. Christ is born, and millions of minds so grow and cleave to his genius that he is confounded with virtue and the possible of man. An institution is the lengthened shadow of one man.[7]

In an episode of the original "Star Trek" television series, a Vulcan starship and its entire crew was destroyed. The crew of the starship *Enterprise* offered their condolences to Mr. Spock, their first officer, who was also a Vulcan. When one commented on the number of Vulcans lost, Mr. Spock replied he found it curious in humans that they consider the loss of many individuals to be so much worse than the loss of one, for destruction of any individual is already the ultimate loss. Individuals do not become more valuable qualitatively merely because they have been multiplied quantitatively. It is rather curious that we attribute to the aggregate of individuals greater value than to its its individual components. We submit to the group mentality and allow the society to dwarf the individual: the group acquires such great identity and value that the group displaces the individual's worth. It is difficult, if not impossible, for the member to enjoy genuine individuality and social acceptance and a sense of belonging. The individual seems to shrink so in value that his or her identity becomes depersonalized, reduced to a mere number. The person feels helpless and, consequently, hopeless. What difference does one person make? What can one person do?

> Insist on yourself; never imitate. Your own gift you can present every moment with the cumulative force of a whole life's cultivation; but of the adopted talent of another you have only an extemporaneous half posses-sion. . . . Every great man is an unique.[8]

What one person can do is to genuinely live according to freely chosen and embraced values and goals. But, of course, we are great imitators and long not only for fulfillment but also for security. Because we long for acceptance by and security within the group, we often compromise our personal values, believing that we can get others' love and acceptance only by being what they want us to be. In the end, we have a society full of individuals all scrambling for the approval of a select set of members who are, themselves, at the mercy of the preferences of their select set of members, and on it goes. But we have put the cart before the horse: as long as we love and accept another only if they do (or think or believe) as we think they should, then what we value is not really the other person, but rather the person's values. When we forsake our deeply held, individual beliefs to earn the love of another, we are dis-appointed to find that it is not we who are now loved, after all. A few lucky individuals who learn that lesson early in life avoid the wholesale capitulation that most of us perform in our efforts to be loved and accepted for ourselves, as if we had ever seriously cultivated our selves.

Uniqueness has never been celebrated in ethical system building—at least not by and for the individuals who have lacked positions of power or influence in the social structures or in the field of professional philosophy. As I noted in the intro-duction, uniqueness is not only not encouraged, it is strongly discouraged in the name of order and stability. But maintaining order and stability exact a great price from the members of any group. When the individual eventually discovers that group thought no longer works, he or she is severely disillusioned. I learn that I was not discouraged from being myself because the

other, socially approved, identity was really better but because
the society would run more smoothly and we would all act in a
more predictable and orderly fashion. But I can add one
encouraging word. Despite the repeated conditioning and
implicit demands to conform that bombard us from all sides, we
all still experience, inside, that stirring that reminds us that we
must eventually face the question of our purpose in living and
that even claims of perfect conformity to an exterior standard
will not quiet its existence. The self must eventually offer an
accounting of its lifetime and its values.

Because the individual experiences the self with greater or
lesser force throughout a lifetime, one tackles ethical system
building with an urgency that depends on one's age or stage
of development in life. Some people seem to struggle relent-
lessly from the moment they are born, while others begin
building only at the end of a long life. What is common to the
experience, though, is knowing that I have to have been more
than a mere placeholder in my culture.

The Purpose of Life for the Species

The prospect of answering the question about our purpose in
life as a species threatens and horrifies many people who associate it with tampering with nature—genetic engineering run
amok. It conjures up images of weird monsters and barely recognizable humanoids populating our future societies. Our
fear of science keeps us ever vigilant, eager to solve problems
and willing to allow a small degree of external control or tampering to achieve solutions, but also keeps us constantly alert
to the danger of technology's unleashed and unchecked powers. However, the refusal to direct our own development is, in
itself, a choice of the direction our development will take:

> At some time in the future we will have to decide how
> human we wish to remain—in this ultimate, biological
> sense—because we must consciously choose among the
> alternative emotional guides we have inherited. To chart
> our destiny means that we must shift from automatic

control based on our biological properties to precise steering based on biological knowledge.[9]

We have the means, scientifically and technologically, to actively direct the development of our species. But, of course, that is only half the means. We need to know in which direction we should move and how we should develop as a species—knowledge that lies in the domain of ethics. There was probably a time in our species' history when the predicament was precisely reversed: we possessed the ethical acumen but lacked the scientific and technological skills, a condition less dangerous to our group than our present one. We are now sorely underdeveloped in ethics but equipped with the technology to destroy life on our planet.

We seem to suffer simultaneously from underdeveloped and overinflated egos. We are too unsure and afraid to claim responsibility for directing our own evolution, but we presume that our species represents the pinnacle of intelligent life. Robert Nozick, a contemporary philosopher, took a good-natured jab at the pervasive influence of modern humankind's anthropocentrism:

> Human beings . . . justify the eating of meat on the grounds that the animals we kill are too far below us in sensitivity and intelligence to bear comparison. It follows that if representatives of a truly superior extraterrestrial species were to visit Earth and apply the same criterion, they could proceed to eat us in good conscience. By the same token, scientists among these aliens might find human beings uninteresting, our intelligence weak, our passions unsurprising, our social organization of a kind already frequently encountered on other planets. To our chagrin they might then focus on the ants, because these little creatures, with their haplodiploid form of sex determination and bizarre female caste systems, are the truly novel productions of the Earth with reference to the Galaxy. We can imagine the log declaring, "A scientific breakthrough has occurred; we have finally discovered haplodiploid social organisms in the one- to ten-millimeter range."[10]

This is not to say that our species is not important and worthy of our attention and care. The state of our species is really more important than we individual members realize: we have historically taken for granted that our development as a species requires no intervention or work on our part—that only our individual growth and development requires that. We are learning, through the positive influence of science, that groups of self-conscious beings can become self-directed. Until we trust our sense of direction, our species will simply drift and just hope that we move along the right path. But eventually our species will have to answer the question of our purpose in life. Then we must look honestly at our short-comings and strengths and consciously choose—a value judgment—the direction of our development. We must choose either to cooperate and trust or to compete and distrust. Humans can choose to live together peacefully and work together constructively. Peace and prosperity in our future require commitment and work in the present.

The Purpose of Life for the Individual

We answer the question of our purpose in life many times. Its form changes to reflect our stage of life, but each time it asks us what we are and why we have lived as we have. The teenager who thinks appearing different from his or her peers is virtually life-threatening is not yet sufficiently separate and independent to feel comfortable doing original thinking. When, at forty or so, that person may feel ready to behave differently, he or she will find that the question will arise again and with more force. We cannot accomplish what we are not yet equipped to undertake. The ethical overhaul that I propose here requires that individuals be sufficiently mature, both emotionally and intellectually, that the overhaul can be meaningful to them. People do not mature physically or emotionally at the same rate, neither do they mature ethically at the same rate. The successful person is not who gets through the process the fastest or who creates the most sophisticated or elegant system of ethical beliefs: the successful person frees himself or herself to formulate answers that will make sense of his or her own life. The process will unfold in a unique pattern and at a different pace for each person who takes up the challenge. One need not feel pressed into uncomfortable haste, either intellectually or emotionally. The suggestions I offer are for all to pick over and pick from, bearing in mind that the issues addressed in preceding chapters have been intended for readers struggling for autonomy and the right to be autonomous. These complicated issues have far-reaching implications for one's emotional life and stability and are intended for mature readers. Most of us have already survived the various stages of conformity and socialization that leave us conditioned, civilized, and, usually, severely crippled. In his first book, *Love,* Leo Buscaglia presents a parable in which animals establish a school. To make it a proper school, they decided on a common curriculum.[11] All animals had to learn to perform all the tasks performed by all the species, so all species learned flying, tree-climbing, burrowing, and so forth. The birds excelled at flying, but broke their beaks during the burrowing exercises. The small ground animals fell to the earth when they attempted to fly, sustaining, in some cases, severe injuries. None of them could excel at everything. At commencement, the valedictorian species excelled at nothing, but sustained the fewest injuries from its education.

Many of us may believe that the crippling effects of our socialization have outweighed the advantages, but the pattern need not be repeated for all generations. We cannot abolish the natural stages of socialization that humans experience, but we can nurture the spark of creativity and uniqueness in every individual. This nurturing will threaten our sense of safety in numbers, but it is possible to spare those who will come after us some of the pain and disillusionment we have all been through as we dug our way out of traditional wisdom. We can even spare ourselves and our contemporaries some of the fear and threats that hinder the search for and assertion of our own ethical systems. We must forsake old ways and superstitions, which is always difficult to do, but most of us must face the process sooner or later, because the question of our purpose in life cannot be put off forever. We can never claim, "I was just following orders."

How to Help Oneself and Others Become More Ethical

Becoming more ethical is the practical issue, of course. Understanding ethics has no value unless it enables us and those around us to behave more ethically. Therefore this last section addresses helping people become more ethical. We have seen that we acquire our ethical beliefs under the strong influences of many factors—some rational, some nonrational, some irrational—and our competing drives. With so many different factors, how can we ever hope to create a more ethical world? It takes real work to make oneself over and to help others to do the same, but the beginning, of course, costs more energy and time than the maintenance. We can replace the destructive habits that have crippled and limited us with constructive methods of thinking and interacting that will benefit everyone and encourage all persons' best sides to flourish. However, it will not be as easy as handing out a new set of rules and thinking up novel ways to punish noncompliance. First we need to acknowledge what does and does not work, and then apply it where we can create a better world.

The largest contribution an individual can make to uplifting the ethical climate of his or her society is to act in the most ethical way he or she can and thereby model for the society another way to live than the quite selfish and immoral stance that people often take toward one another. People need to see good ethics in action before they will believe that it is truly possible, much less desirable. Like most people, I no doubt misremember much of my childhood, but I will recount here an incident that I remember vividly because it reveals how ethical values are evoked in us by others' expectations, encouragement, and confirmation.

When I was growing up, my town had only one radio station. The morning announcer broadcast the local news and the weather forecast. Many people listened before leaving for work or school. On one morning, the announcer said that he had had a flat tire on his way to the station and had to pull over to the side of the road. He was wearing a new watch, an anniversary gift from his wife. To avoid scratching the watch, he had taken it off and carefully placed it on the curb before repairing the tire. After driving on to work, he realized that he had left the watch on the curb. So, when he went on the air, he announced the exact location where his watch could be found and he asked any listeners passing by the spot to please stop and pick up the watch and then to let him know where he might come to collect it. He repeated the location of the watch (just north of a major intersection), and then reported the news. Several minutes into the following program he came on the air again and thanked the listener who had picked up the watch and driven to the radio station so that the announcer need not go all day without his watch. The truly amazing thing about the incident is that no one in my hometown considered it amazing! Good ethical behavior, like bad ethical behavior, springs from habits that have been long internalized and either supported and rewarded or discouraged and punished.

In Victor Hugo's *Les Miserables,* the protagonist, Jean Valjean, is taken to the home of a cleric for shelter and a meal. While everyone else is sleeping, Valjean creeps out of the house, taking all the silverware. When he is apprehended by the police for other activities and the stolen goods are noticed, the police return him to the home of his former host. Valjean, of course, assumes that the man will smugly accuse him and rejoice that he is being punished for the theft. But, the cleric actually protects him by claiming that he had given him the silver. He even chides him for forgetting the candlesticks! That unexpected kindness and mercy makes Valjean reconsider his treatment and mistreatment of others.

How do we begin to create behaviors that encourage and nourish the goodness in others and ourselves instead of killing it? The simple answer is slowly, deliberately, and with great effort. We have to become more conscious of the importance of such behaviors and let go of destructive habits and ways of thinking that discourage ethical behaviors. Each of us contributes to the moral climate of our communities, and often, through unconscious actions and unexamined attitudes, we help support the distrust and prejudice of our communities. All habits are tough to break, and only deliberate and conscious redirection of our behavior over a long time will be effective.

Of course, the first illusion that we must abandon is the misconception that if everyone acts ethically, then they will all act the way I think they should. Because acting ethically requires adherence to one's individually determined system, it cannot guarantee any particular outcome. Universal compliance with authentic ethical systems will not guarantee universal harmony and agreement. We no doubt will continue to disagree on many major issues, but if we were all ethical beings, we would work on accepting and compromising and understanding rather than waging war against those with whom we disagree. Despising and destroying those with differing ethical views does nothing to improve the world but much to compromise one's own morality. If you want a more ethical world, then you must do what you can to create the conditions that promote authentic ethical behavior. You must accept the inevitable differences between even ethically good individuals. The goal is to free the individual's ethical self to become the author of its own actions and not the mere conduit of others' desires and plans. We can take several concrete steps to promote our own and others' self-development and to create a positive ethical force.

1. Overcome the conditions that are known to cripple one's own free exercise of self and will, such as addictions, ignorance, and unhealthy and overly dependent relationships. These conditions limit a person's ability to see and think clearly and to act on his or her own desires and choices. The individual may be so completely influenced by someone or something else that all real choice and self-direction is virtually impossible. Keeping oneself focused and in control is the first and foremost requirement to promote ethical behavior. I cannot behave ethically unless I am in control, and I cannot do that while enslaved to other people, addictive substances, others' approval, or my self-imposed, vincible ignorance.

2. Spend time sorting through your own beliefs. Get to know what you think about how your world works and how you have intellectually solved ethical problems until now. Subject the system to a major scrutiny. Consider your ideas about human happiness, your goals and plans for self-realization, and how these

ideas have shaped your notions of ethical responsibility. Once you really see the forces that have been holding you back, you can act as a self-directed and self-directing agent. The process should not appear so threatening after overcoming the hurdles listed above. However, for most people, learning to recognize one's true opinions and feelings about issues is an incredibly challenging task. Because we have all learned to experience and feel what others have insisted on, identifying what is genuinely our own is very difficult at first. Then we must evaluate those beliefs to sort out which of our genuinely felt and believed ideas are effective and worthy to be retained in our systems. It takes much time to do this, but, after all, what other comprehensive process can be accomplished in less time or with less effort? If you keep in mind the magnitude of the endeavor, you can avoid being frustrated by unrealistic expectations.

3. Acknowledge the inevitable differences between sincere thinking individuals as they develop their ethical systems. Aristotelian logic has created our Western preference for two-valued logical systems, the natural conclusion from the following postulates formulated by Aristotle: A is A (Principle of Identity), A is not not-A (Principle of Noncontradiction), and A or not-A (Principle of Excluded Middle). In other words, every object either has a particular quality or does not have that particular quality, but it cannot both have and not have the quality, nor can it both lack a quality and lack not having the quality. Hence we tend to see the world in black and white, with little, if any, gray. When we examine ethical dictates and question their truth value, we expect each theorem to have one and only one truth value: the theorem is either true or false—not both and not neither. If one system accepts a particular theorem and another rejects it (the theorem is true in one system and false in the other), we assume that one system must be right and the other wrong. By unconsciously applying our Aristotelian logic, we draw a conclusion that directly opposes individual

thought and action. We Westerners hate paradoxes and are reluctant to approve any process that creates one. We must consciously suspend the belief that, for us all to be correct, we all must embrace exactly the same ideas and the same standards. We must allow differences in the axioms that ultimately yield conflicting ethical theorems. We can all be right, even if we lack universal agreement about our conclusions. But allowing for those large gray areas is, for most of us, counter-intuitive and will be accepted only after overcoming great intellectual reluctance.

4. Encourage and reinforce independent thinking and judgment on others' parts (and your own). Once you successfully jump the logical hurdle in the previous step, you can approach others' work as valid, or at least interesting and nonthreatening, even when it differs radically from your own. We need the encouragement and support of others in this endeavor, and positive feedback provides as great an incentive to persist as the negative feedback provides to give up and think like the group. We must make conscious efforts to avoid the manipulation and bargaining that we have all learned to promote harmony. Sameness must be rooted out and replaced with cooperation and mutual respect, a more realistic and mature approach. Conformity would, likewise, need to be discarded as the model of true citizenship and social virtue. The world in which independent, mature ethical thinking is actually encouraged will look very different from the world we inhabit.

A New World

To return now to the person who is searching for his own ethics, we can offer some words of consolation and hope. We need not continue along that road paved ages ago, full of potholes and conflicting signposts. Although habits of thought may change slowly and only with great effort, they can change.

The individual can retain a place within the group while maintaining an independent ethical system. Ethical maturation can be initiated (or resumed, if there has been a long stagnation) at any time in one's life. Many discover the trigger to be the onset of the mid-life experience. Discomfort is natural and necessary, but not fatal. As in any growth process, the person experiences a strange, uncomfortable spurt of growth, which gives way to familiarity and at least some comfort.

What is most important is to see that ethical system building is a natural human function to be undertaken by every person, not just the intellectually elite. The systems we create will lack the pseudo-infallibility that we mistakenly attribute to our current systems, but that emotional demand was always unrealistic for human endeavors. In the genuine new world, we must be willing to give up our expectations of perfection, limitless fun, and effortless virtue. Society has proven an oppressive foe to individual thought, but we have also proven to be our own worst enemy by embracing the illusory pleasures that society offers us for a price. We have also been each other's worst enemy by being threatened by each other's independence of thought. We cannot demand freedom for ourselves without extending the same courtesy to others, but many of us still find that exchange threatening.

It is still (and will always be) easier to follow others from day to day, year after year, but, beneath the surface, answering the question about the purpose of our lives is lurking, waiting for its turn. The question does us a favor by prodding us to not waste time because our time is limited, and none of us is sure how much he or she has. The picture is really an optimistic one, because every person can develop a genuine, unique role and belief system. Like Dorothy in the film, *The Wizard of Oz*, we always have the power to get home but do not know it. However, we have lacked a trusted guide to remind us of our inherent powers. Such guides are rare, and so the truth for each of us gets mangled, misinterpreted, and just plain lost along the way.

> Let a stoic arise who shall reveal the resources of man and
> tell men they are not leaning willows, but can and must
> detach themselves; that with the exercise of self-trust, new

powers shall appear . . . and that the moment he acts from
himself, tossing the laws, the books, idolatries and customs
out of the window,—we pity him no more but thank and
revere him;—and that teacher shall restore the life of man
to splendor and make his name dear to all History. It is
easy to see that a greater self-reliance—a new respect for
the divinity in man—must work a revolution in all the
offices and relations of men; in their religion; in their education; in their pursuits; their modes of living; their
association; in their property; in their speculative views.[12]

Like the other arts, the art of ethics is a creative process
challenging each person to develop his or her own mode of
expression. Although each serious work of art can be judged
on its form or expressiveness, the creative effort must be
respected as having value in itself. Genuine art combines originality, discipline, talent, and training. These factors direct and
color the creation of ethical systems, and so allow each system
to bear the special stamp of its creator and to stand as a
unique, valid expression of his or her values. The question of
the purpose of our existence is too profound and too personal
to be answered through one pat, conditioned answer. Only a
rich and endless variety of creative answers can explain why
each of us is here and how each individual answers the challenge to live as a human should.

Notes

Introduction

1. Eric Mount, Jr., *Professional Ethics in Context* (Louisville, Ky.: Westminster, John Knox Press, 1990), 18, 22.

2. Ibid., 22.

Chapter 1

1. William James, "The Present Dilemma in Philosophy," in *The Writings of William James*, ed. John J. McDermott (New York: Modern Library, 1967), 362.

2. Leo F. Buscaglia, *The Sounds of Love*, a lecture delivered in Boston in March 1988, available on audiocassette from Nightingale-Conant Corporation.

3. John Wisdom, "Gods," in *Classical and Contemporary Readings in the Philosophy of Religion*, ed. John Hick, 2nd ed. (Englewood Cliffs, N.J.: Prentice-Hall, 1970), 429–45.

4. Thomas D. Davis, "Those Who Help Themselves," in *Philosophy: An Introduction through Original Fiction and Discussion* (New York: Random House, 1979), 106.

5. Harriet Martineau, *How to Observe Morals and Manners* (New Brunswick, N.J.: Transaction Publishers, 1989), 57.

Chapter 2

1. Jean Piaget, *The Moral Judgment of the Child* (Glencoe, Ill.: Free Press, 1948), 1.

2. Ibid., 4–5.

3. Ibid., 7–8.

4. Ibid., 16–17.

5. Donald Vandenberg, *Being and Education: An Essay in Existential Phenomenology* (Englewood Cliffs, N.J.: Prentice-Hall, 1971), 70.

6. R. D. Laing, "The Obvious," in *To Free a Generation,* ed. David Cooper (New York: Collier Books, 1968), 30.

7. Ibid.

8. Ibid., 31.

9. Ibid., 32.

10. William G. Perry, Jr., *Forms of Intellectual and Ethical Development in the College Years* (New York: Holt, Rinehart and Winston, 1968).

Chapter 3

1. Eric Mount, Jr., *Professional Ethics in Context* (Louisville, Ky.: Westminster, John Knox Press, 1990), 16.

2. Ibid., 24.

3. Alfie Kohn, *The Brighter Side of Human Nature* (New York: Basic Books, Harper Collins, 1990), 13.

4. William James, "The Sentiment of Rationality," in *The Writings of William James,* ed. John J. McDermott (New York: Modern Library, 1967), 339.

5. Ibid., 337.

6. Kohn, *The Brighter Side of Human Nature,* 41.

7. Ibid., 44.

8. Morton Hunt, *The Compassionate Beast* (New York: Doubleday, Anchor Books, 1990), 49–51.

9. Martineau, *How to Observe Morals and Manners,* 73–74.

10. Mount, *Professional Ethics in Context,* 19.

11. Hunt, *The Compassionate Beast,* 109–16.

12. James, "The Present Dilemma in Philosophy," in *The Writings of William James,* ed. John J. McDermott (New York: Modern Library, 1967), 365.

13. Ibid., 366.

14. William James, "The Will to Believe," in *The Writings of William James,* ed. John J. McDermott (New York: Modern Library, 1967), 726.

Chapter 4

1. Aldous Huxley, *Brave New World and Brave New World Revisited* (New York: Harper and Row, 1932), 169.

2. Ibid., 170.

3. Ibid., 183.

4. Ibid., 184.

5. G. Peter Fleck, *The Blessings of Imperfection* (Boston: Beacon Press, 1987), 7.

6. Ibid., 3.

7. Jean-Paul Sartre, *No Exit and Three Other Plays* (New York: Vintage Books, Random House, 1955).

8. Walter A. Kaufmann, ed., *Existentialism from Dostoevsky to Sartre* (New York: Meridian Books, 1956), 378.

9. Thomas D. Davis, "The Land of Certus," in *Philosophy: An Introduction through Original Fiction and Discussion* (New York: Random House, 1979).

Chapter 5

1. Daniel C. Dennett, *Elbow Room* (Cambridge: Bradford Books, MIT Press, 1984), 76.

2. Thomas D. Davis, "A Little Omniscience Goes a Long Way," in *Philosophy: An Introduction through Original Fiction and Discussion* (New York: Random House, 1979).

3. Austin Fagothey, *Fagothey's Right and Reason*, rev. by Milton A. Gonsalves, 8th ed. (St. Louis: Times Mirror, Mosby College Printing, 1985), 35.

4. Morton Hunt, *The Compassionate Beast* (New York: Doubleday, Anchor Books, 1990), 44.

5. Ibid., 21.

Chapter 6

1. Lewis M. Andrews, *To Thine Own Self Be True* (New York: Doubleday, 1987), 16.

2. Ibid., 17.

3. Ibid., 8.

4. Ibid., 20–21.

5. *One Day at a Time in Al-Anon* (New York: Al-Anon Family Group Headquarters, 1988), 368.

6. Edward O. Wilson, *On Human Nature* (Cambridge: Harvard University Press, 1978), 3.

7. Ralph Waldo Emerson, "Self-Reliance," in *Essays by Ralph Waldo Emerson* (New York: Thomas Y. Crowell, 1926), 42–44.

8. Ibid., 60–61.

9. Wilson, *On Human Nature,* 6.

10. Ibid., 17–18.

11. Leo F. Buscaglia, *Love* (Thorofare, N.J.: C. B. Slack, 1972).

12. Emerson, "Self-Reliance," 55–56.

Bibliography

Andrews, Lewis M. *To Thine Own Self Be True*. New York: Doubleday, 1987.

Buscaglia, Leo F. *Love*. Thorofare, N.J.: C. B. Slack, 1972.

———. *The Sounds of Love* (audiocassette). Nightingale-Conant Corporation.

Davis, Thomas D. *Philosophy: An Introduction through Original Fiction and Discussion*. New York: Random House, 1979.

Dennett, Daniel C. *Elbow Room*. Cambridge: Bradford Books, MIT Press, 1984.

Dewey, John. *The Quest for Certainty*. New York: Capricorn Books, 1960.

Emerson, Ralph Waldo. "Self-Reliance." In *Essays by Ralph Waldo Emerson*. New York: Thomas Y. Crowell, 1926.

Fagothey, Austin. *Fagothey's Right and Reason*. Revised by Milton A. Gonsalves. 8th ed. St. Louis: Times Mirror, Mosby College Printing, 1985.

Fleck, G. Peter. *The Blessings of Imperfection*. Boston: Beacon Press, 1987.

Hunt, Morton. *The Compassionate Beast*. New York: Doubleday, Anchor Books, 1990.

Huxley, Aldous. *Brave New World and Brave New World Revisited*. New York: Harper and Row, 1932.

James, William. *The Writings of William James.* Edited by John J. McDermott. New York: Modern Library, 1967.

Kaufmann, Walter A., ed. *Existentialism from Dostoevsky to Sartre.* New York: Meridian Books, 1956.

Kohn, Alfie. *The Brighter Side of Human Nature.* New York: Basic Books, Harper Collins, 1990.

Laing, R. D. "The Obvious." In *To Free a Generation.* Edited by David Cooper. New York: Collier Books, 1968.

Martineau, Harriet. *How to Observe Morals and Manners.* New Brunswick, N.J.: Transaction Publishers, 1989.

Mount, Eric, Jr. *Professional Ethics in Context.* Louisville, Ky.: Westminster, John Knox Press, 1990.

One Day at a Time in Al-Anon. New York: Al-Anon Family Group Headquarters, 1988.

Perry, William G., Jr. *Forms of Intellectual and Ethical Development in the College Years.* New York: Holt, Rinehart and Winston, 1968.

Piaget, Jean. *The Moral Judgment of the Child.* Glencoe, Ill.: Free Press, 1948.

Sartre, Jean-Paul. *No Exit and Three Other Plays.* New York: Vintage Books, Random House, 1955.

Vandenberg, Donald. *Being and Education: An Essay in Existential Phenomenology.* Englewood Cliffs, N.J.: Prentice-Hall, 1971.

Wilson, Edward O. *On Human Nature.* Cambridge: Harvard University Press, 1978.

Wisdom, John. "Gods." In *Classical and Contemporary Readings in the Philosophy of Religion.* 2nd ed. Edited by John Hick. Englewood Cliffs, N.J.: Prentice-Hall, 1970.

Index

A

Abraham and Isaac, 29
Absolutist approach to ethics, 15–17, 35, 41
Alcoholics Anonymous, founding of, 133
Altruistic actions
    false dichotomy set up between selfish acts and, 124–25
    legal requirements to perform, 62
Altruistic tendencies, development of, 58–59, 68
Andrews, Lewis M., 152
Approval of others as reward for subscribing to their beliefs, 32
Aristotelian logic, 145
Aristotle
    logical principles of, 145
    motivations for people's choices analyzed by, 98
    view of highest good of, 92
Art of ethics, 148
Attitudes, discipline and training's effect on, 71–72
Autonomy in ethical beliefs, 40
    developing, 81
    first step toward 43
    rehabilitation of criminals at cost of, 63
Authorities in ethics. *See* Experts, ethical
Authority
    as basis of ethical theorems, 19–20
    inauthentic use of, 27
    individual's right to defy, 104
    reconciling ethical development and, 30–32
    response to, programming for, 23
Authority figure, guilt in disobeying, 27–30
Axioms
    absorbed from parents, 68–69
    choices of, 7–15
    culturally adopted, entire people influenced by, 14
    damage from, 7
    disrupted selection of, 11–12
    examination of, 6
    formed from conclusions to sorted data, 75
    parallel of intuitive beliefs and, 5
    symmetry in, 7
    top down (socially imposed) transmittal of, 11

B

Bad Samaritan statutes, 62
Beatitudes, various sects embracing values in, 64
Behavior
    axiom-directed, 12–14
    caused by us, freedom as, 112
    ethical, 26–31, 73, 122, 144
    judged by motive versus effect, 13, 125–28
    mechanical, 53–54
    negative, parents' demonstration of, 70–71
    random, 111–12